ABSOLUT SEQUEL.

ABSOLUT SEQUEL.

{ THE ABSOLUT ADVERTISING STORY CONTINUES }

RICHARD W. LEWIS

PERIPLUS

Published by Periplus Editions with editorial offices at 364 Innovation Drive, North Clarendon, Vermont 05759 and 130 Joo Seng Road #06-01/03, Singapore 368357.

Library of Congress Control Number: 2005904077

ISBN: 0-7946-0401-3 (hardcover)

ISBN: 0-7946-0331-9 (paperback)

Distributed by

North America,
Latin America & Europe
Tuttle Publishing
364 Innovation Drive
North Clarendon, VT 05759-9436
Tel: (802) 773-8930
Fax: (802) 773-6993
info@tuttlepublishing.com
www.tuttlepublishing.com

Japan
Tuttle Publishing
Yaekari Building, 3rd Floor
5-4-12 Ōsaki
Shinagawa-ku
Tokyo 141 0032
Tel: (03) 5437-0171
Fax: (03) 5437-0755
tuttle-sales@gol.com

Asia Pacific
Berkeley Books Pte. Ltd.
130 Joo Seng Road
#06-01/03 Olivine Building
Singapore 368357
Tel: (65) 6280-1330
Fax: (65) 6280-6290
inquiries@periplus.com.sg
www.periplus.com

Grateful acknowledgment is made for permission to reproduce the following material:

ABSOLUT MILES
Bitches Brew © 1970, Abdul Mati Klarwein, Courtesy of the Mati Klarwein Estate 40cm x 80cm, Oil on posterboard. Private collection.

ABSOLUT KEROUAC
2004™ Jack Kerouac by CMG Worldwide, Inc./*www.CMGWorldwide.com*

ABSOLUTLY
Courtesy of June Newton / Maconochie Photography, London

MULIT
Special thanks to Arun Nemali . . . without whose contribution this film would have been un-listenable.

First edition

09 08 07 06 05   10 9 8 7 6 5 4 3 2 1

Designed by Eric Janssen Strohl, Eric Baker Design Associates, New York, New York

Printed in Singapore

DEDICATED TO STAN LEWIS

my ABSOLUT DAD

TABLE OF CONTENTS

introduction

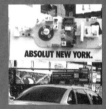

I love you Mulii.

INTRODUCTION

NOW, WHERE WERE WE?

Ten years ago—1995—I wrote the ABSOLUT BOOK. I promise I won't indulge in the annoying middle-aged habit of telling you how fast the time has passed. If you're old enough to drink Absolut vodka, you know how fast the time has passed. (And if you're not old enough, you're even luckier, but don't drink until you're twenty-one. Seriously. What's the damn hurry, anyway?)

BERNIE THE RABBIT.

Yikes! It is an absolutely different world. A decade ago we seemed so innocent—or maybe just less guilty. What have we seen, heard, tasted, drunk, laughed, and cried at since? The "rational" exuberance of the Internet mania—which led to the inevitable Internet meltdown . . . and rebirth. Monica Lewinsky's transformation from a naïve coed at Lewis and Clark College to a different kind of celebrity, and the New York Yankees winning four World Series championships, including the 2000 Subway Series against my much-maligned Mets. (How many Flushing hearts were broken by that too-sensitive lug, Armando Benitez?)

On the darker side, we've been through the tragedy of September 11 (with the subsequent real fear of flying—sorry, Erica Jong), the greed of the Enron Gang, the comedy of the Florida electoral system, and disappearing WMDs in Iraq.

On the personal side (in no particular order) my beard has turned gray, making me appear academic—and older. (Check the inside back cover for proof of both.) We have a rabbit in the Lewis house: her name is Bernie. She's imperturbable. We can all learn from that.

I've had two Lewis Bat/Bar Mitzvahs for Amanda/Sam, respectively. My daughter Ariane is in medical school so there should be someone to take care of me when I'm truly

old. My wife, Isabel, has gotten skinny (lots of vegetables, lots of treadmill) and more beautiful. They all still laugh—or moan—at my jokes. Including Bernie.

Nearly all my friends got divorced. Since you know who you are, I won't name names. Doesn't anything last anymore? (Recently seen in a USA Today piece about evolving wedding vows: " . . . as long as we continue to love one another." Translated: as long as it lasts.)

Ah, there's a segue. Absolut lasts. Absolut advertising lasts. The advertising campaign is twenty-five years old and still going. And if it isn't great every day, it still tries to be great every day. And it's still the single most significant connection between the vodka and the consumers who buy the vodka.

We recognize that very few consumers run out to a bar to order a drink or race to their wine and spirits shop to buy a bottle immediately after seeing an ad. (That's probably a good thing. If advertising were so powerful, it would be difficult to get anything else done!) We have to stack up Absolut "credits" in people's minds so that we can "cash them in" when they're ready to make a purchase. And the ads are our way of building our "credit line" with consumers. (We're also aware that only one of three adults drinks spirits. It doesn't hurt if the other two think the Absolut

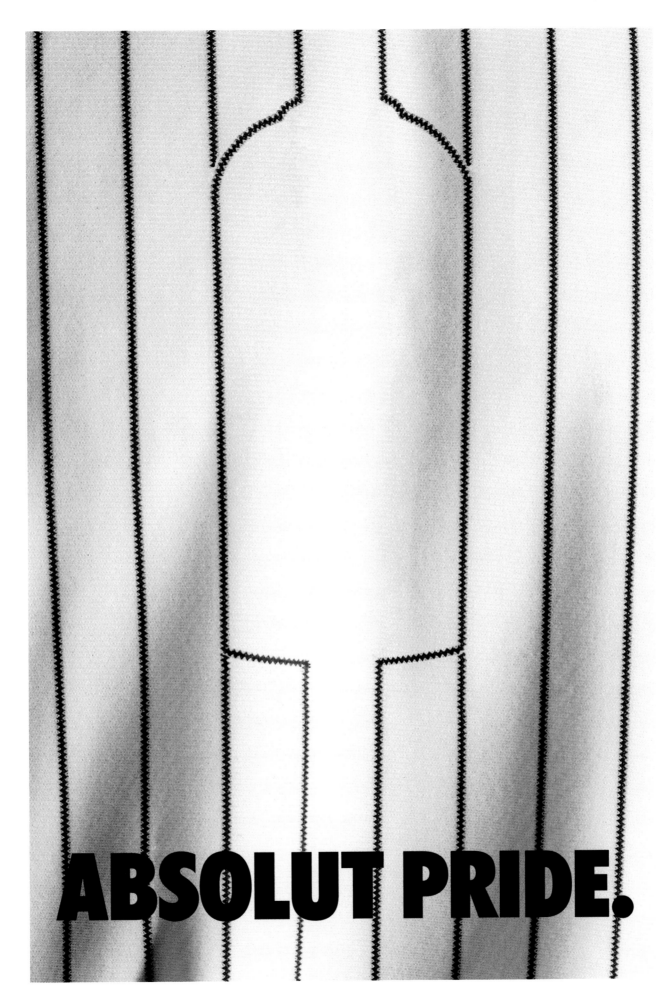

ABSOLUT PRIDE.

ABSOLUT MANILA.

ABSOLUT KITSCH.

drinker has good taste.)

Published in 1996, the first ABSOLUT BOOK was a hit because the advertising was a hit. At TBWA I saw the hundreds of consumer ideas that came in over the transom—and through the mail—some of them as clever as our own. Clearly, we had reached the point that every advertising person dreams about—consumers were thinking about our products almost as much as we were.

Of course, the lawyers warned us to not even look at our mail for fear we would be accused of "stealing" somebody's idea. But I like opening the mail—just ask my wife. Anyway, how am I supposed to know there's an aspiring Absolut ad inside until I open it?

We also knew that college dorm rooms across America were festooned (a great visual word: think July 4th banners and ribbons) with students' favorite Absolut ads. (So we weren't surprised to see Meadow Soprano's Columbia University dorm plastered with them in 2000. The set designer for the HBO series was only replicating the college experience. This wasn't a product or advertising placement. This was a reflection of real life!)

ABSOLUT BOOK was a great adventure, chronicling the campaign's first fifteen years. (If you haven't read it yet, it's still worth the $30. Not to mention $8.99 on eBay,

although I don't make a single krona on those copies.) It was encyclopedic, probably including 99 percent of that era's print ads. Plus the inside story of what made the campaign tick. And a few ounces of Richard Lewis humor.

This book has a somewhat broader mission.

Today, Absolut is recognized as one of the world's most valuable brands. In fact, in 2002, Forbes magazine called it the world's biggest luxury brand—ahead of BMW, Tiffany, and Gucci. While I don't think of Absolut as a luxury brand, who am I to argue with Forbes?

To drive this growth, TBWA and The Absolut Company have greatly diversified their advertising and marketing programs over the last ten years. While magazine ads are still the hallmark, the heavy lifters, for Absolut, we have also developed effective advertising in many other media: cinema, outdoor, and the Internet. By effective, I mean it increases the real estate in consumers' minds that Absolut is worth buying, giving, or at least admiring.

In the past decade, Absolut has become a worldwide brand. TBWA markets it in nearly 50 countries, and it is available in 150 countries. Our staff talks to local consumers around the world in the hope that we can create ads that will "speak to" all of them. (The ads always appear in English, the world's business language, even in places like Brazil, Turkey, India, China, and England.) We determine which ads best serve a particular market, usually including those with a local accent. It doesn't take a marketing genius to figure out that residents of Manila will have a special connection to ABSOLUT MANILA.

But we've found that consumers are more similar than dissimilar as we travel from Rome, New York, to Rome, Italy, or Paris, Texas, to Paris, France, or New Delhi, Pennsylvania, to New Delhi, India; OK, you get the idea. They are urbane, social, cultured, fun-loving, outgoing (when they're not in-going), experimental, experiential, young, middle-aged, and old folks.

We'll also meet the fans, the people who Goran Lundqvist, former president of Absolut, described as "drinking the advertising as much as they're drinking the vodka." Over the past decade there has been a steady growth in trading Absolut ads for (what else?) other Absolut ads. This commerce takes place mostly among students, but also between adults with time on their hands. As dozens of the ads appeared just once or in a single magazine, we've kept these searchers really busy.

Entrepreneurs have started clubs to organize the trading. When eBay was born in 1995, "Absolut" was a favorite search. Today, over 500 Absolut tchotchkes are for sale at any given moment, including special bottles, bar equipment, T-shirts, posters, and, of course, ads. Some for as little as a dollar! There are even used copies of ABSOLUT BOOK. (I promise I've never posted anything.)

Later on in the book, you'll get to meet some of these collectors and learn firsthand what makes them such Absolut (advertising) fanatics.

Or, more delicately, Absolut ambassadors. Because these aren't teenaged girls screaming for the Beatles; or budding

philatelists examining commemorative stamps through a magnifying glass. They are somewhere in between, sharing the exuberance of the former and the determination of the latter as they search for their Absolut rarities.

These ads didn't create themselves. We fuel the Absolut engine with the creative brains of the best—and craziest—talent in the TBWA network. So throughout the book I'll try to give credit to the many who deserve it, and bring a few of these characters to life, at least for the time they're on the screen.

The big promise department: this book will include Absolut stuff that you have not seen before—because it hasn't appeared in the USA (or any other major market). Or it hasn't appeared anywhere because it was created especially for this book. Therefore, don't scratch your head when you come upon something new; rather, smack your lips as your Absolut world expands.

While the Absolut advertising campaign has 2,000 faces, it's still a singular idea. A big Absolut bottle. A two-word headline starring ABSOLUT and finishing with a word that denotes a state of excellence, a mood, a place, a person real or imagined, a powerful linkage to the arts, amber fields of winter wheat—or anything else I might have forgotten.

It's George Plimpton, Zelig, the Chameleon Man all rolled into one. It's aspirational, inspirational, and recreational. It's Andy Warhol, Marilyn Monroe, and John and Yoko. And it's you—and your mom.

One final note: This isn't brain surgery. Or as brain surgeons might say, "Relax, this isn't advertising." So, throughout, I promise not to overcomplicate the simple. Or be weighty when I can be svelte. Or preachy when I can be conversational. I hope to be more Tom Thumb than Tom Peters. After all, this is supposed to be fun.

CITIES

chapter one

AS I THINK BACK TO THE BIRTH OF THE ABSOLUT CITIES CAMPAIGN IN 1988 with the arrival of ABSOLUT L.A., I can't help but smile. It was such a simply brilliant idea by two advertising characters, Tom McManus and Dave Warren. Speaking to them sixteen years after the deed, there's still this sense of, "Hey, we were just having fun. Who knew it was smart?"

DAVE WARREN AND TOM McMANUS, CIRCA 1988.

ABSOLUT L.A. L.A. changed all the campaign's rules. Like ABSOLUT WARHOL, it opened the doors to nearly everything we've done since. No actual Absolut bottle. No Absolut vodka inside. No complimentary description of the drinker or the vodka. Just attitude, a finger in the cultural pie, and a tongue pressed firmly in cheek. I'm not certain if it became my favorite ad because it was so skin-shedding for the campaign, or because I've been asked so many times for my personal favorite (as if it mattered) that I needed a snappy answer.

Not surprisingly, ABSOLUT L.A. also fulfilled its marketing mission: it increased Absolut's business in Los Angeles and California, helping the brand surpass Stolichnaya the following year. It made us realize people wanted a home team—in this case, ad—to root for. And it instilled in us the idea to "Think local, act local," a variation of the marketing voodoo maxim, "Think global, act local." Since the debut of L.A., we have created about 250 city ads in the campaign—covering six continents. (We're still working on the McMurdo, Antarctica, ad—summer population: 1,500—which will give us all seven.) We have covered some cities more than once. From a purist's standpoint I don't think it's a great idea. I've always been a subscriber to one man, one vote. Therefore, I also believe in one city, one ad.

ABSOLUT BOSTON But you can't unplug the idea machine when it's humming along. So when someone says, "Hey, I've got a great idea for Los Angeles," we can't ignore it. (And people in the ad business hardly ever shout, "I have a pretty good idea.") As much as I relish breaking the rules, I can't very well complain when people come along and break my rules.

There are also so many great cities that haven't been saluted with a single ad. It isn't always for a lack of trying. Sometimes failure is more interesting than success. Two examples come to mind: Baltimore and Detroit.

Baltimore is a terrific town I got to know because my daughter Ariane attended Johns Hopkins, graduating last year. Without shilling for the city's tourist board, it's rich in history: Francis Scott Key wrote the "Star Spangled Banner" as a prisoner in Fort McHenry; there's the great harbor, Little Italy, and Fells Point neighborhoods. Edgar Allan Poe lived, wrote, and died there. It was Babe Ruth's hometown and Cal Ripken Jr.'s only team. Not to mention the setting for movies by writer/directors Barry Levinson and John Waters, and on and on.

Enough already, I'm showing off. But we couldn't find, or I should say agree, on a universal Baltimore ad that the clients loved. You probably wonder what that means. I know I do. But imagine yourself sitting in a room with people from Philadelphia; New York City; Greenwich, Connecticut; Stockholm; and Johannesburg. Some people know a little bit about B'more. Some don't. Everyone wants to idealize it, though, to live up to the trust the city places in us. So, maybe a crab claw shaped like the bottle isn't good enough.

Detroit presented a similar headache. An obvious temptation was to connect Absolut with "Motor City," using

ABSOLUT BOSTON.

ABSOLUT BOSTON.

some aspect of automobile manufacture. But client and industry guidelines "steered" us away from cars altogether, because of the drinking and driving association. Anyway, you can imagine an Absolut assembly line.

After a few more fits and starts we came up with a Motown idea that nearly made it out of the studio. The ad would have shown a 45rpm record with a Motown label featuring "Absolutely Love" by The Martinis.

However, we needed permission from the Motown people. We had an "in": the Motown label was owned by Universal Music, which was owned by Seagram, then the importer of Absolut. We figured we could get the permission for a song. (Sorry, couldn't resist.)

But just the opposite happened: once we wound our way around their corporate ladder, they asked for $2 million, figuring we were rich and desperate. Well, we were neither. We offered $10 thousand, hoping for the family rate. They just sneered. I implored Edgar Bronfman Jr., then Seagram CEO, to intervene and get us the 99 percent discount. By the time we got his ear, though, everyone else had lost interest in doing the ad. So it simply just ran out of gas.

I'll spare you the stories of our many other failures, except for our one last chance to save Detroit. The concept was inspired by our strategic planner at the time, Larry Geis. Just in case you're not in the advertising business, the discipline of strategic planning was imported from London around 1990.

In fact, Chiat/Day was in the vanguard. Originally dubbed the "voice of the consumer," strategic planners were supposed to represent consumers inside hallowed advertising agency walls. Now they are better described as "insight machines" which the creative department uses to build a campaign.

They try to find a key point of difference in a brand or product and build a strategy around it. Sometimes this is done before a creative team creates. Other times it's retrofitted after a campaign is conceived—to give it a reason for being. Many of these people are exceptionally smart; but they're all very neurotic and suffer from exhaustion, if only because they have to lug around their big brains every day. However, Larry Geis was an exception: he was neither brilliant nor crazy, but down-to-earth, and he was even actually from Detroit!

Larry pointed out the popularity of the Detroit Red Wings, the town's NHL hockey team, and the city's passion for the sport. He said the city's nickname was actually "Hockeytown." (None of us smart-ass New Yorkers knew that.) We checked it out and it was true. While I think we

ABSOLUT PHILADELPHIA.

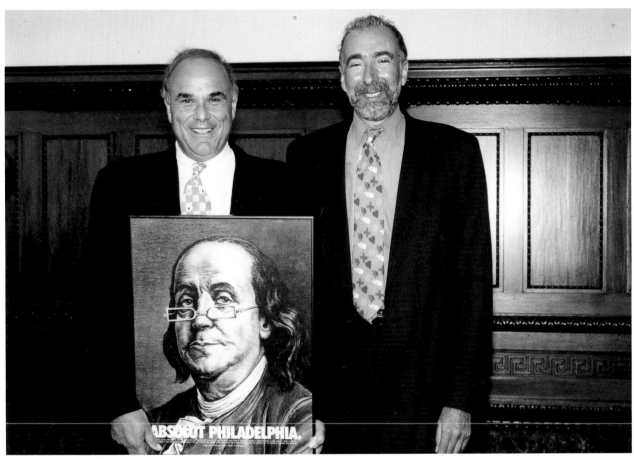

MAYOR (NOW GOVERNOR) EDWARD RENDELL DEMONSTRATES HIS APPROVAL OF ABSOLUT'S HOMAGE TO PHILADELPHIA.

convinced Carl Horton, the Seagram marketing honcho, that we were actually telling the truth about Detroit and hockey, alas, he wasn't a hockey fan. So, pfft, it was dead. We never went back to Detroit.

ABSOLUT PHILADELPHIA Which brings us to Philadelphia. This is a city that is loaded with a backstory—cheesesteaks, the Liberty Bell, the "Iggles," a baby New York, as a recent Southwest Airlines ad branded it.

As the campaign had touched down on nearly all the top ten American cities, I wasn't entirely surprised to be contacted by the Philadelphia mayor's office in 1997. A super-charged assistant there, Phyllis Halpern, working for Mayor (now Governor) Ed Rendell, wrote beseeching us for "their" ad. She wrote and she wrote and she wrote. I should be clear: this was entirely unofficial on her part; she just happened to be one of the mayor's assistants. But she was obviously a Philly booster for life. I liked her immediately, if only because she was a little off the wall, passionate, and dogged.

On the other side of the coin was Carl Horton.

Carl was the VP/Marketing at Seagram, responsible for Absolut once the distribution rights were transferred from Carillon Importers in 1993. Carl confessed early on that he wasn't really wild about being given this responsibility. He reasoned, correctly, that because the Absolut contract with Seagram was so important—size, prestige, and of course money—the people actually working on the brand were going to receive a lot of attention from management.

And Seagram had plenty of management: Edgar Bronfman Jr., the boyish CEO who would later be tarred for the MCA/Universal acquisition and, much worse, the eventual sale of the largely family-owned Seagram to the French water company, Vivendi. Ed McDonnell was the international president given much of the credit for catching the Absolut fish. Steve Kalagher, the U.S. president, was an understated, mild-mannered executive whom everyone liked. Arthur Shapiro, Seagram's marketing chief, actually had sympathy and sensitivity for the advertising (even if his taste was sometimes at odds with ours). Frank Arcella, the U.S. sales head, had a proclivity for big limos and bigger results. And on and on.

It took us a while to appreciate the kind of world Carl lived in at Seagram, a very political distillery, and so different from Michel Roux's Carillon Importers, which, while owned by London's International Distillers & Vintners (IDV), was really his toyshop, and he the toy master.

Back to Carl Horton and Philadelphia. Carl was born and grew up in Philadelphia. This meant he both knew the city and had strong opinions (as he does on every subject) about everything Philadelphia. Carl agreed that a cracked Absolut bottle reminiscent of The Bell was too obvious a choice for the city, the cheesesteak sandwich too pedestrian (and a little sloppy with all that dripping cheese and sautéed onions), and the dome of Independence Hall just too boring. An Agency favorite starred the Mummers, the annual New Year's Day parade of musicians, entertainers, and other characters. But Carl was very clear that the Mummers, despite the tradition, weren't up to his standards.

By the time campaign creator Geoff Hayes conjured up Ben Franklin and his citron-tinted spectacles, it wasn't a moment too soon; everyone was exhausted. But Hayes's ad—his last for Absolut before retiring—was a crowd-pleaser because it was so warm, witty, and totally unexpected.

Naturally, we launched it in Philly at a City Hall reception with His Honor, Ed Rendell, presiding. And everywhere was Phyllis Halpern cheering madly for her ad and her city.

If Philadelphia represented the apogee of municipal boosterism, surely Vail, Colorado, represented its nadir. With the brand's typical spunk and tongue in cheek, we created an ad that demonstrated Absolut's awkwardness on the slopes and why it should never leave the bunny hill. Thus with ABSOLUT VAIL you see a signed plaster cast wrapping the bottle—obviously the result of a graceless wipeout.

Actually, you don't see it—because I can't show it to you. Lovely Vail, Colorado, is, in part, a company town "owned" by Vail Resorts. This includes ski resorts, restaurants, shops, parking lots, "and more" throughout Colorado. When ABSOLUT VAIL debuted, the company demanded Absolut withdraw the ad because Vail Resorts believed that "and more" included the name of the town: Vail. And since Absolut hadn't received "permission" to use the name Vail, and since they didn't appreciate the ad's wit, Vail Resorts decided to sue all of us.

Naturally, this came as a bit of a surprise on every level. We were saluting Vail as an important ski and winter recreation center. TBWA lawyers and Absolut lawyers had blessed the ad without any reservations. And even though we also ran the ad as ABSOLUT KILLINGTON, ABSOLUT ASPEN, and ABSOLUT SUN VALLEY, we didn't hear complaints from any other ski operators. On the contrary, we even received a thank you note from the Aspen folks!

I'll spare you most of the Sturm und Drang that followed.

ABSOLUT COOPERSTOWN.

ABSOLUT SAN DIEGO.

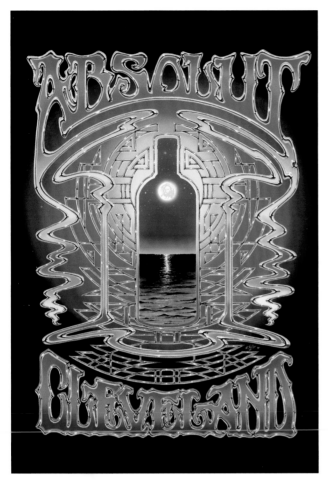

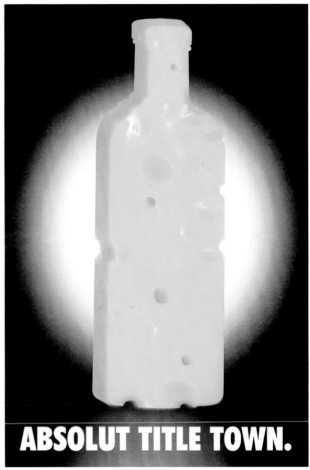

ABSOLUT TITLE TOWN.

A file as thick as the Colorado phonebook grew on my desk. My sister, Valli, and her family (who, coincidentally live just outside of Vail) reported that there was a bit of a backlash in Vail, as townsfolk were uniformly behind Absolut. (Everyone needs a loyal sister.) And the lawyers spent hundreds of hours defending and preparing for a trademark fight. But in the end, business is business, so the case was settled in a Denver courtroom. Among other agreements, we promised to never run the ad again. But if you use your imagination, I'm sure you can fill in the blanks.

ABSOLUT BRONX These ads are good examples of what happens when there are too many baseball fans in an agency. At TBWA, Pete Callaro and I are those fans. Pete joined the company right out of Rutgers in 1990 and proceeded to work for me (or I for him) as an account executive/supervisor/director for nearly a decade. He was a very creative guy, an awful administrator, laughed at my jokes, and introduced me to the Internet.

While Carl Horton despised baseball—"It's like watching paint dry"—he let these baseball ads happen because he accepted that baseball was typically American and wouldn't hurt the business.

As far as execution goes, COOPERSTOWN was the clear winner. The catcher's mask didn't require too much

"surgery" to be Absolut-ized. It looked authentic. You could put it on your face. You could smell the leather, the dirt, and the sweat. Looking back, the bat rack in Yankee Stadium was a bit forced: the bottle shape is too squat, the dugout too trashed.

ABSOLUT SAN DIEGO When I met Nandi Ahuja he was a successful investment banker for Merrill Lynch in London. And he still is. How he came to create this ad is an exceptional story. We never (well, almost never) seek help outside TBWA to create ads. But Nandi was a huge Absolut fan, and just wouldn't take "No" for an answer. He began submitting ideas in the late 90s, refusing to accept our standard legal refrain that we simply weren't allowed to solicit or accept advertising ideas. We weren't even supposed to open our mail in case an idea would sneak through. We were warned that if we later published an ad that resem bled an idea that came over the transom, we would risk being sued and, worse, would probably lose. But Nandi was neither interested in being paid nor being famous; he just wanted to have an ad published in the campaign. Incidentally, his idea was born as ABSOLUT HIDE: as in hide the bottle inside the zebra hide, etc. Nandi reluctantly accepted the ad's transfer to the San Diego Zoo. He submitted dozens of ideas—and still

ABSOLUT DENVER.

ABSOLUT NORFOLK.

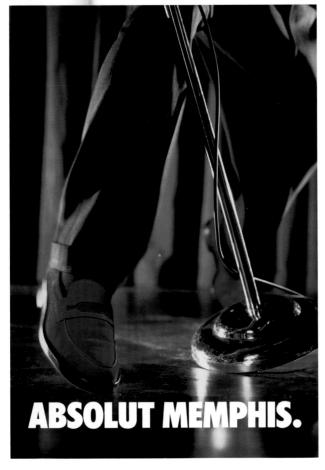

ABSOLUT MEMPHIS.

ABSOLUT ROSWELL.

does—but this one survived our bureaucratic defenses.

ABSOLUT JERSEY OK, I know it isn't a city. And more than a state, it's a state of mind. While it isn't the birthplace of the American diner, it should be. There are more diners in New Jersey than any other state. And New Jersey has more cars per capita than any other state (even California). Sometimes these cars get hungry, or at least the drivers do, and crisscross the state's endless roads to find the perfect . . . diner food. Ham 'n' eggs. Milk shakes. Burgers 'n' fries. Hot turkey sandwiches. Waitresses with plenty of makeup and attitude. We were tempted to headline it **ABSOLUT JOISEY**. I know that was art director Dan Braun's choice. However, some people—none of them from New Jersey of course—felt that this was mildly derogatory, so we stuck with the state's actual surname.

ABSOLUT CLEVELAND Some people still scratch their heads as to how the Rock & Roll Hall of Fame wound up in Cleveland. Rather than join those head-scratchers, let's just accept it. And even honor it. Which is exactly what Absolut did with this artwork created by Alton Kelly, an album cover and poster artist renowned for capturing the Haight-Ashbury, San Francisco look of the 1960's.

ABSOLUT TITLETOWN I'm sure I'd be a Green Bay Packer fan even if my Mother, Janet Lewis, wasn't from Madison, Wisconsin. You'll just have to trust me on this one. So when the Packers won the Super Bowl in 1997, Absolut saluted the cheeseheads there and everywhere. Incidentally, the Packers are the only NFL team publicly-owned—by its fans—yet is the smallest market to have a pro team. The Titletown nickname was coined by Jack Yuenger, an adman at the Green Bay Press-Gazette, during the glory years when they won five titles with Vince Lombardi as the coach.

ABSOLUT DENVER How many ways can you photograph an Absolut bottle so that each tells a different story? Apparently, quite a few.

Denver is justifiably known as the "Mile-High City," because the fifteenth step of the state capitol rests 5,280 feet above sea level. (Although I don't think anyone could tell you just what sea that is. The Red Sea?)

Therefore, it's perfectly logical to show only a portion of the bottom of the bottle as if the remainder was in the stratosphere, figuratively speaking.

ABSOLUT NORFOLK Somewhat at the opposite end of the spectrum breathes **ABSOLUT NORFOLK**. This Virginia city is the home of a major U.S. naval base where the submarines come home to roost. (I learned this from reading too many Tom Clancy novels.) Yes, we altered the tip

of the bottle just a skosh to guarantee that readers would understand exactly where Absolut was peering from. I love these little tailor's alterations.

ABSOLUT MEMPHIS When Pete Callaro pressed for this ad I honestly thought it didn't have a chance. I figured you-know-who's estate would want millions; I figured the client would have a major problem. I figured it's impossible to get a pair of comfortable shoes. I was wrong on all counts.

ABSOLUT ROSWELL If you were a fan of The X-Files, probably the longest-running aliens conspiracy since Stonehenge, then you probably have a place in your heart for women with red hair and the citizens of a little town in New Mexico (pop. 35,005) that have their heads in the clouds more than most of us.

ABSOLUT WOODSTOCK Maybe I'm cheating here, a bit. But just here. This ad was created for the thirtieth anniversary of the 1969 festival of music and peace. But Woodstock is a real town, of course, even though the actual concert on Max Yasgur's farm was held in Bethel, New York.

ABSOLUT LATIN AMERICA

Just call me Fodor. As the Absolut brand and business spread around the globe, nearly all of the local marketers expressed an interest in having their city or country or culture become a part of the campaign. Their enthusiasm was something akin to fielding a team for soccer's World Cup. Or having your country represented at the Olympics. I don't think I can overstate the passion that "locals" everywhere had for Absolut and its advertising. Because it was the story of "little guy" success—Swedish vodka takes on the United States and wins!—that inspired many of these people. While I never heard anyone sing, "If I can make it there, I'll make it anywhere," Frank Sinatra's "New York, New York" resonates everywhere. And Latin America was no exception.

The countries of Latin America are often mis-lumped together. You've heard it a thousand times: the people struggle almost continuously for economic growth, political stability, and self-respect. But peel away the layer of headlines and you quickly see the kind of fun-loving, family-hugging, hard-working people that you find, well, everywhere. And unlike North America, which has been "civilized" for a mere 400 years, many of these countries can boast civilizations that go back another 1,000. So these countries are rich in history, culture, and national icons. And there's a vibrant spirit evident in the lively

ABSOLUT MEXICO CITY.

ABSOLUT XOCHIMILCO.

ABSOLUT GUADALAJARA.

KIM WIJKSTROM AND ANN STOKES.

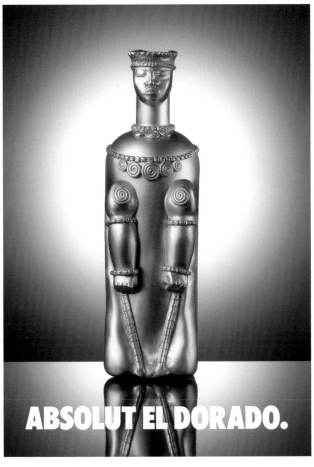

ABSOLUT EL DORADO.

ABSOLUT CARACAS.

nightlife throughout the continent.

Enter the Swedes. In 1998, Absolut's communications manager, Ann Stokes, was determined to initiate a new city series for Latin America. And when Ann is determined to do something, it's best to go along with her—or be prepared to be blown away by the tsunami whirlwind that surrounds her.

Prior to joining Absolut, Ann held a variety of different marketing and public relations jobs in Stockholm, staying long enough in each to impress on people that she was a woman who got her way, not through guile but just force of personality. (Ann also lived in Melbourne, Australia, for a few years, and used to describe her then-marriage to an Aussie cowboy quite comically on her Swedish-oriented public radio show. I'm sure it was riveting for the seven other Swedes who lived in the country.)

Ann's partner in crime at TBWA was Kim Wijkstrom. Short for Joachim, Kim had joined TBWA a year earlier in the Account Planning Department. However, he failed to impress one of the super-brains who led the department that month, and was fired. At his exit interview he was informed he didn't have "the soul of a planner." God bless him.

But Kim was a smart, likable, well-traveled and educated gentleman and, coincidentally (really), he was Swedish. So I

rescued him. I figured I could find a place for him in Account Management, and I knew it would annoy the planning director who had fired him. Together, the two were the most dynamic team of Swedes since the Bergmans.

ABSOLUT SANTIAGO Santiago is surrounded by the Andes mountains, yet is one of the most modern and contemporary cities in South America. The funicular that journeys up Cerro San Cristobal to Parque Metropolitano offers riders incredible vistas. However, as Wijkstrom admits, he was in over his head as an art director, and the cable car seems a touch too big for the city over which it hovers.

ABSOLUT MEXICO CITY Chapulin is the Aztec word for grasshopper. And Chapultepec, logically, is the home of the grasshoppers. At 1,600 acres, Chapultepec Park is the largest park in Mexico City—the largest city in the world. Twice the size of New York's Central Park, the park is surrounded by lakes, museums, a zoo, and great places to eat. It's truly an everyday refuge for Mexicans—and grasshoppers—of all ages.

ABSOLUT XOCHIMILCO Pronounced zo-CHE-mil-ko, Xochimilco is a series of canals south of Lake Texcoco where the ancient city of Tenochtitlan (today's Mexico City) was built. It's one of the few remainders of the original Aztec civilization. See, the Aztecs practiced a form of

ABSOLUT 90-60-90.

ABSOLUT AMAZÔNIA.

ABSOLUT PANTANAL.

ABSOLUT SÃO PAULO.

hydroponic agriculture by creating "floating islands" where they grew crops such as corn and cocoa. So, there's lots to learn when one is selling vodka.

ABSOLUT GUADALAJARA Lars Olsson Smith, Absolut's "king of vodka," adorns every real bottle of Absolut in the form of a small silver medallion. L. O. Smith was a very important person in Absolut history because he created the system of continuous distillation that's still in use today. Simply, it's a series of columns that help separate and remove the impurities encountered in distilling vodka. This rectification process makes Absolut the purest vodka on Earth. Back to Guadalajara: It's the home of charreria, the art of horsemanship—another one of L. O.'s skills. We couldn't resist adorning him with the traditional head garb, el sombrero.

ABSOLUT MAYA The stone carvings left behind by the Mayans tell many different stories: great battlefield victories, biographies of their rulers, as well as the more mundane tales of domestic life and proper cocktail recipes.

ABSOLUT EL DORADO Legend has it there was once a Colombian tribe that was so rich that its chief was ritually painted in a fine gold dust. ("OK, dear, we've painted the bathrooms and the children, so you're next!") He was nicknamed El Dorado, "The Golden One," by the Spanish Conquistadors. Of course, the gold-laden tribes of Colombia have never been found—that's why they call it a legend—but that doesn't mean we can't keep looking.

ABSOLUT CARACAS We called them snow cones when I was a kid. In tropical Caracas, Venezuela, the locals beat the heat at the raspao stands to be found on nearly every street corner. The ice from these crushers—with flavored syrups added—is an Absolut treat for both young and old.

ABSOLUT 90-60-90 Did you know that Venezuela is famous for its beautiful women? Trust me, it is. And these women always seem to be finalists in international beauty pageants. This lovely, diamond-studded crown pays tribute to these women. I have faith that you, dear reader, will figure out the meaning of the headline. I can't tell you everything.

ABSOLUT BUENOS AIRES Jorge Luis Borges told a story about a Buenos Aires café. It had a door that led to a street in Prague, which ultimately ended in the Piazza Navona. His point: Geography is defined by culture and imagination—not by mere physical borders. This concept seems natural in Buenos Aires, the most European of the Latin American capitals.

ABSOLUT CAIPIROSKA The traditional spirits drink of Brazil is the caipirinha. It's made by adding cachaça, a fermented sugar cane, to muddled (not confused) limes and sugar over ice. It's actually quite yummy. However, a caipirinha made with a premium vodka such as Absolut is called a caipiroska. Even yummier.

ABSOLUT AMAZÔNIA The araras caninde macaw is indigenous (and hails from) the Amazon region. The noisiest birds anywhere, they're also faithful to one mate all their lives. (There must be a connection: "Get back here you silly bird! Where do you think you're going?") Their faces even turn red when they get angry. Our research has also turned up an odd transformation of their plumage during cocktail hours

ABSOLUT PANTANAL The Pantanal is a huge, land-locked river delta stretching from the south of the Amazon basin to just east of the Andes. (Check your Rand McNally if you doubt me.) The tuiuiú (great Scrabble word) bird is one of the more famous inhabitants, and is believed to be quite fond of spectacular sunsets. While ornithologists have no explanation for this unusual flocking formation, they do attribute it to the bird's refined social skills.

ABSOLUT SÃO PAULO Founded almost 500 years ago, and today the business capital of Brazil, São Paulo, is often referred to as "Seattle of the South" for the 148 days of the year that the garoa—drizzle—descends upon the city's pedestrians.

ABSOLUT CANADA

The folks in Canada approached "city ads" from a different perspective: they decided not to do them. I believe they just weren't ready to tackle the big question, "How do we represent Vancouver? (And Toronto, Montreal, etc.) As an American, I would have forwarded lots of snappy answers. Surely, Larry Geis's HOCKEYTOWN could have found a second life and a second home in VANCOUVER. And I have to believe there's a lobster out there willing to die for HALIFAX. But the Canadians said this was all a little cheesy and came up with a different idea: a series featuring the beauty of the Canadian landscape.

ABSOLUT SEVEN SEVEN was actually a band of seven Canadian artists who self-formed in 1920 to glorify the beauty of the Canadian north, painting the majesty, scenery, and spirit of their land. This painting is a tribute to them. The seven artists were Franklin Carmichael, A. J. Casson, L. L. Fitzgerald, Lawren Harris, Edwin Holgate, A. Y. Jackson, Frank Johnston, Arthur Lismer, J. E. H. MacDonald, and Frederick Varley. Even if you weren't

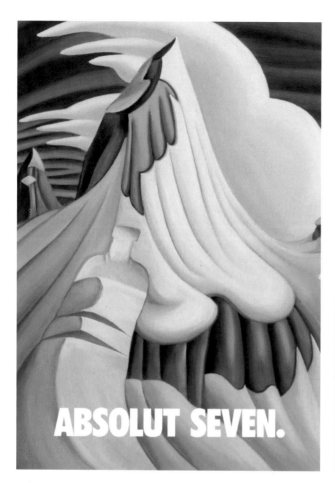

ABSOLUT SEVEN.

ABSOLUT CHINOOK.

THE SHARPE BLACKMORE PARTNERSHIPS. ABSOLUT COUNTRY OF SWEDEN VODKA AND LOGO, ABSOLUT, ABSOLUT BOTTLE DESIGN AND ABSOLUT CALLIGRAPHY ARE TRADEMARKS OWNED BY V&S VIN AND SPIRIT AB. ©1996, V&S VIN & SPIRIT AB.

ABSOLUT BACKBONE.

ABSOLUT RUSH.

counting, that had to feel like more than seven. That's because once the original seven left their Toronto homes to vacation in the north, their ranks soon swelled because there was such an outpouring of support for what became the first Canadian art movement to honor this previously untapped chunk of Canada. If you can imagine, Canadian landscapes were dominated by cows and trees prior to this association. The Group of Seven even had their own pet sayings which they called "algomaxims." One example: "The great purpose of landscape art is to make us at home in our own country." Final point: a key figure who inspired this group, Tom Thomson, died shortly before its formation, but is honored at the Tom Thomson Memorial Gallery on Owen Sound in Ontario.

ABSOLUT CHINOOK I would include this ad even if I didn't like it, just because I enjoy saying "Chinook." While I'm sure Dan Gombos, a budding meteorologist at MIT, knows what a Chinook is, some of you may not. A Chinook is a weather phenomenon that occurs in the Rocky Mountains, which impacts Alberta, Canada, which lies just east. It's a wind that jumps off the mountains after a cold period that can then raise the temperature as much as twenty degrees Celsius (or forty degrees

Fahrenheit) in as little as fifteen minutes. And if you live in Alberta this is a very normal—and frequent—occurrence.

ABSOLUT BACKBONE "If you till it, they will come."

In the Canadian prairies of Alberta, Saskatchewan, and Manitoba, farming is the, you guessed it, backbone of the economy and the cornerstone of what the people are about: hard work, country hospitality, and old-fashioned values. Here, the ground is being tilled, prepared for the next season, by dislodging old roots, turning over leftover plants, and aerating the soil, so there's nice compost for the following year. While this isn't the same as the Absolut recipe, farmers in southern Sweden engage in a similar ritual as they prepare each year's winter wheat.

ABSOLUT RUSH Niagara Falls is one of those natural phenomena that you really can't digest secondhand. And you don't have to descend it in a barrel to feel the rush, hear the power, and smell the excitement. It's also a pretty good place to get wet.

ABSOLUT BOUNTY See, my Halifax idea wasn't so dumb after all. They just made it better. Here, in Peggy's Cove, are several lobster cages awaiting the next trip to sea. These fishermen, like the farmers, live hardscrabble lives in Nova Scotia, New Brunswick, Newfoundland, and Prince

ABSOLUT TOKYO.

Edward Island, so Canadians and other fine tourists, can enjoy these jewels of the sea. Even McDonald's offers a McLobster sandwich up there, which is supposed to be half decent.

ABSOLUT BIRTHDAY This is as close as we're going to get to an **ABSOLUT QUEBEC**. The painting pays homage to Robert Harris's *Fathers of the Confederation*, an 1883 kiss to an earlier conference that laid the groundwork for Canada's nationhood.

ABSOLUT ASIA-PACIFIC

As if Asia and the Pacific Ocean weren't each big enough—the largest continent + the largest ocean—marketers have managed to marry the land and the sea to create a selling territory unrivaled around the globe. Maybe because it takes so long to get from here (New York, Paris, Stockholm) to there (Tokyo, Hong Kong, Sydney), corporations send their hardiest people on Amelia Earhart–type missions to cover these markets.

Back in 2000, the Absolut Company felt ready to put a stake in the ground (and one on the barbie) and sell some vodka in these markets. For years, Asian travelers had been able to enjoy Absolut while visiting the capitals of Europe; many wondered why Absolut couldn't make the journey east. The Japanese shopping the Hermes sales in Paris; the Australians checking out the latest watering holes in London; the Taiwanese exploring the fashion shows in Milan; they all discovered Absolut, but wondered why this international brand wasn't available in their neighborhood. It was these sophisticated travelers: journalists, bankers, ad people, artists, and fashion folk that would light the fire-cracker of Absolut distribution in the East.

Andreas Berggren heard the firecracker explode. Berggren, the son of a Swedish diplomat who served in Russia, was already well-traveled pre-Absolut. He was responsible for Absolut success in Russia and its offspring, and thought it was time to keep moving east. His modus operandi was really quite simple: listen to popular demand, respond quickly, but launch an ad blitz in the Asia Pacific. As the Swedish saying actually goes, "Something, quick, dirty, and perfect."

His idea was to create a baker's dozen of Asia Pac city ads in markets that lacked a distribution structure and product availability, and where even the local agencies were a bit in the dark. "Let the consumers fill in the blanks," he suggested.

We gave this responsibility to the prince of the TBWA

Paris office, Daniel Gaujac. Gaujac took it on as he does everything: barking, but thoroughly disciplined—a general organizing a battle plan that would "get a dozen ads concepted, presented, approved, produced, and ready for publication in five months, the time it usually took to get one ad produced," he quips. To get it done, Gaujac city-hopped, island-hopped, and country-hopped endlessly, briefing, encouraging, and tantalizing each agency office with the possibility of doing the "best" ad of the series, although it was always fuzzy what criteria would be used to determine that lofty title.

By mid spring, seventy-two ideas were whittled down to twelve approvals in a whirlwind meeting of Seagram, Absolut, and TBWA people worthy of a session at the U.N. Despite Asia's notorious reputation for eating global campaigns for breakfast—you know, the expression "Not invented here" was invented there—these Absolut ads clearly crossed the borders intact. By mid summer, they were finished: twelve new Absolut babies.

ABSOLUT TOKYO Originally, this ad took a very different approach. It was going to show a Tokyo subway station with the army of salary men (or as my rich, formerly fat friend, Bob Ingram, says, the ham 'n' eggers) entering the morning train. It was sympathetic but claustrophobic. So we shifted to a visual showing sushi, a subtle selling message that you could EAT sushi but DRINK Absolut (instead of the usual sake or beer).

ABSOLUT KYOTO One could suggest the Tokyo sushi has to come from somewhere. But that would be fishy. The truth about Kyoto is this: in the emperor's garden, the carp are the lucky fish. The more, the luckier. However, the Japanese clients remained unconvinced; you could say they even carped that the agency would be unable to line up the fish in the luckiest manner. No more fish jokes. I promise.

ABSOLUT SEOUL Kites are big in Korea. People fly them for good luck or for fortune telling: by watching their flight, one can foresee the future. Why not? This is especially popular on New Year's Day because citizens want to know what kind of year is coming. The Absolut kite was created by the oldest, most respected kite builder in Korea. But because he was very old and frail, he sent his eighty-five-year-old son to the launch event.

ABSOLUT TAIPEI The Chinese New Year is celebrated on the first day of the first month of the lunar calendar. It begins with the dance of the dragon. This is no ordinary dragon: it requires no fewer than seventeen dragon assistants—every one a "Type A"—to keep it under control. You

ABSOLUT KYOTO.

ABSOLUT SINGAPORE.

ABSOLUT VODKA IS THE SUPREME CHOICE ANYWHERE IN SINGAPORE
ENJOYED NEAT, ON THE ROCKS, OR IN DRINKS AND COCKTAILS.

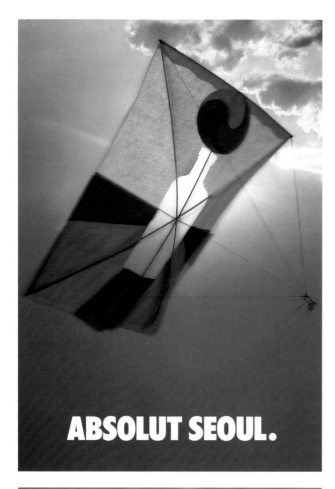

ABSOLUT SEOUL.

ABSOLUT TAIPEI.

ABSOLUT MANILA.

ABSOLUT BANGKOK.

ABSOLUT MELBOURNE.

ABSOLUT AUCKLAND.

may notice that Absolut tongue: it's a sign that the New Year will bring much Absolut vodka.

ABSOLUT SINGAPORE, also known as the Clean City, just might be crazy clean, too. In a city that prides itself on mental, physical, and metaphysical cleanliness, Absolut salutes the desire to polish to perfection.

ABSOLUT MANILA Following World War II, the U.S. Army left thousands of Jeeps behind. Since then, the Filipinos have given them second lives as unique, roving pieces of art. Each family finds a way to individualize their "jeepney" with flags, lights, fruits, and horns. Despite the Absolut ornament shown here, people generally find a better use for Absolut than pouring it into the radiator.

ABSOLUT BANGKOK Bangkok has been home to the floating markets for hundreds of years. Thais come to sell fruit, vegetables, spices, flowers, and other delights. By the way, if you watch the red peppers long enough, they start to wiggle.

ABSOLUT MELBOURNE First, a little education: Melbourne, Australia's second city, is famous for its horse races, which began in the nineteenth century. Melbourne Cup Day is Australia's favorite Tuesday (mine is the Rolling Stones' "Ruby Tuesday"). The entire city grinds to a halt for the great race. The women dress to the nines, particularly when it

comes to millinery. Here, the ABSOLUT MELBOURNE visual isn't merely my favorite Asia Pac ad, it's simply the best Absolut ad, ever, starring a hat. You can quote me.

ABSOLUT SYDNEY Sydney is much more than a city: it's a big, big, beach. Surfing was introduced here in 1915 at Freshwater Beach, just north of the city, by the most famous surfer of all time, Duke Kahanomoku. Seriously. ABSOLUT SYDNEY, incidentally, boasts one of the better, most subtle Absolut bottles of any series.

ABSOLUT AUCKLAND Auckland, New Zealand's largest city, is also known as the "City of Sails." As the country's maritime capital, it claims more sails per capita than any city in the world. This helicopter view of Auckland harbor is an unretouched photo, another example of a naturally occurring Absolut sighting.

ABSOLUT HONG KONG In Hong Kong, you walk your bird down the street inside its bamboo cage. When you take her to the bar (strangely, all the birds are females), there's a special hook to park your bird. Other popular walking pets include bugs and crickets, but the birds are generally in charge.

ABSOLUT BEIJING As Woody Allen said in the movie *Sleeper*, "The nose knows." This adaptation of a traditional warrior's mask is borrowed from a typical Beijing opera.

ABSOLUT SYDNEY.

ABSOLUT VODKA IS THE SUPREME CHOICE ANYWHERE IN AUSTRALIA
ENJOYED NEAT, ON THE ROCKS, OR IN DRINKS AND COCKTAILS.

ABSOLUT HONG KONG.

在中國各地：純伏特加是您至高無上的選擇。
純飲、加冰或調制飲料、雞尾酒：任君盡情享受。

ABSOLUT BEIJING.

在中国各地：ABSOLUT 伏特加是您至高无上的选择。
純饮、加冰 或 调制饮料、鸡尾酒；任君尽情享受。

The man is young (bearded), brave and honest (indicated by the color red), and a general (it's in the helmet).

BACK IN THE U.S.S.R.

I grew up in the 1960s. Cuban missile crisis. President Nixon. Berlin Wall. Iron Curtain. It's hard to give up all those cuddly childhood images. The Commonwealth of Independent States (CIS) was formed after the breakup of the USSR in 1991, forming fifteen independent states. What hasn't changed is the area's taste for vodka. The CIS accounts for 90 percent of the world's vodka production and consumption. The vodka business in Kazakhstan, alone, is as big as the USA's with only one-twentieth(!) of the population. Moscow, a city of nine million, consumes one million bottles daily.

Yet, despite popular misconception, Russians are very savvy drinkers. Their attitude toward vodka is similar to the French attitude toward wine: buy the best you can afford and pour it generously to your guests. And while you wouldn't expect the French to smile and serve California chardonnay, this is exactly what the Russians do when they can.

There were two big reasons why Absolut had a great reputation from the start.

First, Russians respect quality. They've all had patchy experiences with local products, with quality varying from one manufacturer to the next, one batch to the next. They appreciated Absolut's "One Source" message—that every single drop comes from Ahus, Sweden—and production consistency.

Second, because Absolut was many times more expensive than local vodkas, it was a sign of a host's good taste and extreme generosity to serve it.

However, due to an assortment of import barriers, many Russian cities wouldn't have Absolut for sale when the Absolut ad would appear. While this was an inconvenience, the ads ran anyway as a salute to Russian culture.

ABSOLUT MOSCOW This ad is more interesting than it appears. It's a view of the Kremlin from inside the presidential palace. It was photographed under the supervision of a Red Army colonel who advised us we were the first foreigners inside the Kremlin since Napoleon, warning, "You should watch out on your way back."

ABSOLUT K When it comes to Russia's national passions, the runner-up to vodka is chess. And, koincidentally, many

ABSOLUT MOSCOW.

ABSOLUT VODKA IS THE SUPREME CHOICE ANYWHERE IN THE WORLD,
ENJOYED NEAT, ON THE ROCKS, OR IN DRINKS AND COCKTAILS.

of the great Russian chess players have names that begin with the letter K: Karpov and Kasparov, to name two. These two Ks played the longest championship match in the history of chess: five months, forty-eight games, and it ended in a tie!

ABSOLUT 3.2.1...0 Before there was a space race between the two superpowers, this almost top secret photograph from the Baikonur Cosmodrome (shot in 1957), heralded the start of hurling dogs into space. On board was Laika ("Barker" in Russian), the first animal to go into orbit. Americans, however, nicknamed her "Muttnick," as she was aboard Sputnik 2. (You can't say the Russians didn't have a good sense of design.)

ABSOLUT -40° A lot of strange things happen at minus forty degrees: Fahrenheit and Celsius temperatures are equivalent; vodka freezes; wildlife act strangely. In the inner space of Siberia, in towns like Irkutsk, even for the residents, this is cold. The night before our photo shoot, a wild bear ate the reindeer model. The rest of the herd saw the handwriting on the wall and took off. So we had to scramble around in the wilderness, and not the Disney variety, to find our next pretty face. But she is cute.

ABSOLUT POTEMKIN This ad celebrates Odessa, the birthplace of the Russian Revolution, as featured in the brilliant 1925 Sergei Eisenstein film, *Battleship Potemkin.*

The Odessa step scene pictured here is one of the most famous in cinematic history, and has been revered, copied, or saluted, in a number of films, including Brian DePalma's 1987 film, *The Untouchables.*

ABSOLUT YEKATERINBURG Even Russians go on vacation. Usually it's to their dacha in the countryside, where the window treatment industry is huge.

ABSOLUT EUROPE

ABSOLUT WARSAW Poland is another country serious about vodka and protecting its own vodka industry. Vodka drinking is permitted, but vodka advertising isn't. While our Poland cities ads couldn't run in "Polish" publications, they could appear in media that came into Poland, like other European magazines.

Invaders haven't exactly been kind to Warsaw. During WWII, nearly 85 percent of the city was destroyed. Yet a stroll through the old town of "Stare Misto" is like a trip through the Middle Ages. That's because during the period of 1945–1960, the city was painstakingly reassembled from the original plans and drawings. It's difficult, if not impossible, to tell the difference between old and new. Absolut also created the illusion of authenticity with this fountain pump in Rynek Starego Miasta. Does it pump the

ABSOLUT WARSAW.

ABSOLUT VODKA IS THE SUPREME CHOICE ANYWHERE IN THE WORLD,
ENJOYED NEAT, ON THE ROCKS, OR IN DRINKS AND COCKTAILS.

water of life—vodka—or "just" water? You'll have to visit to be sure. (LOT Airlines has daily flights from JFK.)

ABSOLUT GDANSK Gdansk, the cradle of Polish democracy, has always depended on the sea for its livelihood. The Fontana Neptuna was erected in the seventeenth century to honor the Greek god of the sea. I didn't make this up: according to legend, Neptune so loved the city that he made vodka pour from the trident, to the joy of the citizens. However, the city fathers didn't approve (it was probably too difficult to tax), so they surrounded the monument with an iron grate.

ABSOLUT CRACOW At high noon every day, a bugler stands atop the Mariacki Church commemorating the day in 1241 when an arrow fired by invading Tartar forces pierced the throat of the tower lookout, just as he was sounding the alert.

ABSOLUT PRAGUE Prague is Kafka country. Its dark, winding streets have remained unchanged for centuries. Here is where Kafka's character, "the man in the gray hat" (not to be confused with Curious George's "man in the yellow hat") roamed. Prague's shadows, cobblestones, and streetlights paint an environment of magic and suspense.

ABSOLUT TALLINN Some say Estonians sang their way to freedom. In 1988, 300,000 citizens gathered to sing their forbidden national songs in protest. They became the first country to be released from the Soviet Union, ending seven centuries of foreign occupation. The annual All-Estonian Song Festival is an open-air concert featuring a choir nearly 30,000 strong. And leave it to the Estonians to create a very subtle bottle.

ABSOLUT STOCKHOLM As the corporate home of Absolut, I've probably been to Stockholm sixty times. I still get confused walking—and sailing—around. (Don't tell the Swedes, because I always act like I know where I am.) While some may say Stockholm lacks a single defining monument or symbol, I would disagree. The people are connected by the water: Stockholm was built within a unique archipelago of 2,500 islands. An array of waterways connects the city to seemingly any place you'd want to go. Steamboats have been doing the heavy ferrying since the 1800s, carrying the people, the crisp bread, the crawfish, and, of course, the vodka on their journeys.

ABSOLUT ICELAND I'm embarrassed to say that the closest I've been to Iceland was when I bought a Hard Rock Café/Reykjavik T-shirt inside the airport terminal. What a shame. I missed a scene much like the one here, showing the beautiful, yet dangerous mood shifts of the glacier ice and volcanic eruptions. I have been told this is a "real" photograph: absolutely no 0s or 1s were injured by Photoshop during the making of this ad.

ABSOLUT PRAGUE.

ABSOLUT HELSINKI This has to be the only Absolut city ad modeled after a vase; but, oh, what a vase. Aalvar Aalto, a man of many talents (and rich in the letter A), designed the "Savoy" vase for a decorative arts competition held in Paris in 1936. Inspired by a Joan Miro design, this vase changed Aalto's style from his earlier square designs to the organic style that made him famous.

ABSOLUT OSLO Skiing comes naturally to the Norwegians: they invented it 4,000 years ago. If you take a fifteen-minute tram ride out of Oslo, you'll come upon Holmenkollen, the home of the annual World Cup Ski Jump held in July. (But bring your VISA card, because Norwegians love flying through the air, but they don't take American Express.)

ABSOLUT DUBLIN Ireland has produced more first-rate, world-class writers per capita than any other nation in the world. With a population under four million (the size of Kentucky), the Irish can claim Joyce, Wilde, Swift, Shaw, Yeats, Beckett, O'Casey, Thomas, Synge, and . . . Why don't you put this book down and read some real literature.

Absolut has just scratched the surface of saluting the world's cities. If your town hasn't yet achieved Absolut notoriety, don't despair. It's just a matter of time.

ABSOLUT DUBLIN.

ARTISTS

chapter two

ART IS IN OUR GENES. OR IS IT IN OUR JEANS? TWENTY YEARS AGO, ANDY

Warhol was infatuated with Absolut, the bottle. Anyone familiar with Andy Warhol's

career wasn't surprised. Warhol was intrigued by pop icons: Brillo Soap Pads, Marilyn

Monroe, Levi's jeans, and of course, Campbell's Soup cans. But Warhol's infatuation had

an effect on Absolut's marketing that it didn't have on Campbell's tomato soup. As far

as I know, Campbell's didn't subsequently go out and commission a thousand artists to

provide their interpretations of the soup can as Absolut did for its bottle. (There hasn't

even been a paean to tomato rice, a far more interesting soup.)

ABSOLUT HIRST.

ABSOLUT WARHOL.

ABSOLUT BARCELÓ.

But Campbell didn't have Michel Roux, either, the visionary CEO of Carillon Importers, the company that introduced Absolut vodka to the USA, and the man who, more than anyone before or since, made liquor cool—by recognizing the power of art to transform Absolut and the power of Absolut to transform art.

Roux's vision was simple. Get the art world to adopt Absolut, to make it its naked subject for every artist from Warhol to the students at the School of Visual Arts taking Drawing 101, and the benefit to the brand would be enormous. Absolut would become part of the conversation, the buzz. Hopefully, artists and their friends and followers would drink Absolut, too.

But we wouldn't just use art as a business accelerant. Sure, art could help us sell more vodka, but the idea was actually much bigger. Art would ultimately change the brand: as a supporter of the art world and by joining its causes, by becoming a standard of and an advocate for creativity and, later, freedom of expression, Absolut would become more controversial, more passionate, more argued about—and more memorable. Those are pretty high aspirations for a bottle of vodka.

How did Absolut transform the art world? Simple: (nearly) every artist wanted, aspired, or agreed to become an Absolut artist. Not everyone said "Yes." Some deals didn't happen because the artist insisted on being paid more than Absolut was willing to pay. But no one declined because Absolut was too commercial and they were, too, uh, serious. In the past decade, Nam Jun Paik, Damien Hirst, Louise Bourgeois, Francesco Clemente, Ross Bleckner, Chris Ofili, and dozens of other prominent artists have said "Yes" because Absolut has become a respected partner in the art world. Not an interloper. Not the hungry beast. Not trying to get rich by hoarding fledgling artists' early works, only to sell them once they're successful. Imagine, advertising that's promoting art, as well as the brand. For advertising, that's practically honorable.

By the late '90s, Absolut was beginning to be associated with a new generation of drinkers who patronized new venues: bars, cafés, and clubs.

At the same time, a new generation of artists was emerging, capturing the drinkers' imaginations. For the most part, these artists were not art school grads. They were characters, exploiting the same media that tried to exploit them: creating and enjoying bad publicity, sometimes shocking, sometimes just clownish, but always newsworthy. These two groups, consumers and artists, even shared a vodka—Absolut, of course. ABSOLUT ORIGINALS was born from the intersection of these spirited artists and newby adults.

ABSOLUT OFILI.

ABSOLUT TROCKEL.

ABSOLUT SAUDEK.

Absolut vodka and Absolut advertising were first introduced in Europe in 1992. Some of the distributors were already aching for an Absolut artist to ignite their markets—they had seen Warhol's impact in America. France pushed for Combas, a well-known Parisian artist; England lobbied for Peter Blake, famous for the Beatles' Sergeant Pepper cover. Instead, we made a conscious decision to wait until Absolut was sufficiently popular to warrant an artwork.

TBWA's Daniel Gaujac and his counterpart from Absolut, Martina Westin, raced across Europe lassoing this new breed of artists to appear in an Absolut collection. Gaujac realized that the exposure the campaign would offer would appeal to the artists. He didn't need a system of agents and procurers to find them, either. He and Martina would do it themselves. Gaujac was born into the "family of Maeght," the creator of the St. Paul de Vence art foundation, so he felt eminently qualified to do this. (And besides, he's French, there's nothing he can't do.) And in truth, he probably was. Gaujac had grown up in this milieu, so he felt perfectly comfortable ferreting, negotiating, and consummating with this other world.

ABSOLUT HIRST Damien Hirst was first. Hirst was already famous—even I had heard of him—as a British Bad Boy. A London artist, he made headlines practically week-

ly. He's a painter, sculptor, installation artist, curator, director, restaurateur, and World Cup singer. He attracted the media heat earlier in the decade by placing a four-foot tiger shark in a formaldehyde tank and titling it *The Physical Impossibility of Death in the Mind of Someone Living*. Hirst likes formaldehyde ("It's dangerous but it looks like water") and employed a similar device for Absolut. An Absolut drinker, as well, Hirst's response to the loaded question, "You don't trust people who don't drink?," was "Absolutely."

Hirst threw a party to celebrate his Absolut ad at his London restaurant, Pharmacy. It was a heady time for the brand. Goran Lundqvist, Absolut's popular and life-loving president, quipped, "I just signed a contract with Damien Hirst and John Irving [the American author] to do Absolut ads. Guess what business I'm in."

Certainly, Lundqvist wasn't in the conventional business of "selling" vodka. He was leading a company that wanted to inspire a whole new generation to feel creative, and surely, different from their scotch- or wine- or anisette-drinking parents. Always quotable, Lundqvist concluded, "The consumers are drinking the ads as much as they're drinking the vodka."

ABSOLUT BARCELÓ Once Hirst signed on, the door was open to the pantheon of European artists. In Spain, Miquel Barceló, was an obvious choice. A partial recluse,

ABSOLUT DELVOYE.

ABSOLUT BALKA.

ABSOLUT MARISCAL.

Barceló worked half the year in Africa, purposely staying out of the limelight. Initially, Barceló hated the idea, even tearing up an Absolut brochure to demonstrate his disdain. But minutes later he reassembled the shards from the same brochure and created a triptych image of an African marketplace.

ABSOLUT OFILI This might actually have been Chris Ofili's first commissioned piece of art. Ofili, too, was reluctant at first to work with any brand. What convinced him, he says, was a rap song by a much-admired KRS-1 that ran over a Nike television ad. This gave him the "permission" he needed to work with Absolut.

Ofili's painting utilized his trademark: elephant dung pieces, supplied by the London Zoo. Clearly, Ofili uses the dung to challenge people's concept of both art and shit, and the transformative powers of each. (Ofili's art raised quite a stir in New York City in 1999. Mayor Rudolph Giuliani threatened the Brooklyn Museum with a loss of city funding if they didn't remove his art from their "Sensation" exhibition. He didn't succeed. Art is supposed to make you crazy.) Ofili won the prestigious Turner Prize in Britain in 1998.

ABSOLUT TROCKEL Rosemarie Trockel will tell you she

failed as an art student but succeeded as an art teacher at the Köln art school in Germany. Trockel will also tell you— and demonstrates here—that "with a simple horizontal line one can divide the universe." She created an endless video loop showing a woolly striptease that reveals and then redresses the bottle.

ABSOLUT SAUDEK Born in Prague, Jan Saudek compensates for an unhappy childhood with a happy adulthood as a skilled and styled photographer. Predominately using black and white ("I couldn't afford color"), Saudek shot this "Spirit of Absolut" featuring a young model who's strong and independent. Some wayward British readers of *Time* magazine protested the model's apparent lack of underwear. We had to testify that it wasn't the case. Some people just have nothing better to do.

ABSOLUT DELVOYE Wim Delvoye is a Belgian sandblaster: Sand is one of his favorite media. Recognizing that bottles, too, are made of sand, he traveled to Jordan for these authentic desert sandscapes. Try and find the camel with five legs.

ABSOLUT BALKA This little lighthouse is actually a Morse-coded bottle of Absolut. Warsaw-born Miroslaw Balka is an admirer of Samuel Morse, the inventor of the

ABSOLUT GAGNERE.

ABSOLUT HOLLEIN.

eponymous code and the first international language. Imagine that: growing up in Poland in the 1960s, admiring an American inventor from the 1830s. Small world. Poland is a big deal vodka producer and consumer. Balka was actually pretty brave to do an Absolut ad, which was deemed treacherous in some circles.

ABSOLUT MARISCAL Javier Mariscal will be the first person to tell you that his drawings are terrible. But when Absolut rang his studio bell in Barcelona, he asked, "What took you so long to find me?" Mariscal simply lacks all pretension and thinks life should be a little more fun. Bravo!

ABSOLUT GAGNERE Olivier Gagnere, the French designer, decided to place furry rings on the Absolut bottle to provide both warmth and a softer texture to his cold, hard steel bottle. He wanted to challenge our expectations—and reveal something new in something very familiar.

ABSOLUT HOLLEIN Hans Hollein is an Austrian architect and artist who relaxes by taking a bath. (Which reminds me of creative director Patrick O'Neill's homily, "You never feel worse after taking a shower.") As an Absolut artist, he trumped himself, adding the bottle to Hans Haus, a building he designed. While Hollein considered living the life of

the solitary artist, he is too intrigued by the real, physical world to just paint, and sculpt, and soak his days away.

ABSOLUT FAIRHURST Angus Fairhurst is a charter member of the so-called Young British Artists. He attended Goldsmiths College where he met Damien Hirst. For Absolut, he employed an oddball medium, plastic label tags, which he discovered while shopping. Fairhurst was intrigued/irked by a particular label on a dress, which read: "Hello, let me introduce myself, I was made with you in mind, I was made for living in and I am fun, I am fearless, I am the best, so wise up and try me." I think Fairhurst is saying, "You'd have to shoot me before I buy this dress."

ABSOLUT KANA Katerina Kana is a Greek photographer interested in both fashion and art. One sells an idea, one sells a product, she believes. Her ABSOLUT KANA does both. Her friend Louise posed for the photo that symbolizes the female spirit, maybe even the Face of Vodka. Incidentally, Katerina Kana is an artist whose last name fits snugly inside her first name. I notice these things.

ABSOLUT CATTELAN Cattelan, a true Absolutist, doesn't take his art or himself too seriously. He claims the mouse wasn't too eager to crawl inside the bottle. But Maurizio

ABSOLUT FAIRHURST.

ABSOLUT KANA.

ABSOLUT WOLGERS.

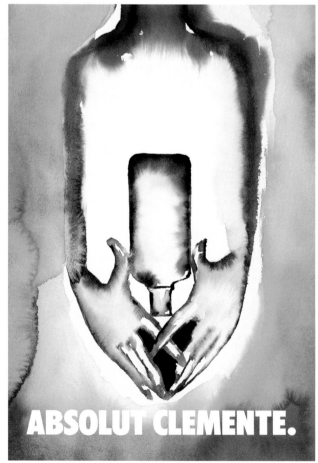

ABSOLUT CLEMENTE.

ABSOLUT BEN.

ABSOLUT BLUE NOSES.

Cattelan charmed him in, anyway. He promised fame, fortune, and a good meal back in Milan. Promises, promises.

ABSOLUT WOLGERS There would be no Dan Wolgers if there were no Marcel Duchamp. (At least, there would be no ABSOLUT WOLGERS) Born in Stockholm, Sweden, Wolgers was inspired by the modern art original, Marcel Duchamp, and his un-Absoluted bottle rack. Wolgers provided the missing link, seventy-five years after the fact.

ABSOLUT CLEMENTE Francesco Clemente believes the world is inhabited by tourists and refugees; he considers himself a tourist. Born in Naples, he has lived in Madras, India, and resides in New York. Clemente was a compatriot of Warhol and Haring, and a poet who collaborated with Robert Creeley and Allen Ginsberg. ABSOLUT CLEMENTE is a product of his virtuoso watercolor technique incorporating two Absolut bottles. It debuted in a retrospective of his work at New York's Guggenheim Museum in October 2000.

ABSOLUT BEN Ben is another Marcel Duchamp champion. Duchamp and John Cage were the grandfathers of the art movement Fluxus, which currently counts Yoko Ono as a member. I didn't know any of this before I met Absolut; and am not certain I know it now. But when

people, particularly parents, tell me their children have been inspired to learn about or even create art, because of Absolut, I know what they're talking about. It's contagious. Ben, meanwhile, is a funny little man who doesn't take any of this too seriously. A wise man.

OEDIPUS WRECKS

When Andy Warhol passed the Absolut baton to Keith Haring in 1986, by suggesting to Michel Roux that Haring should be the next Absolut artist, a number of things happened. The most obvious: Michel Roux's risky, singular idea—an Absolut bottle, transformed into a Warhol bottle, and advertised as such—was on the verge of becoming a series. A dot was about to become a line. Roux was vindicated, the Absolut "persona" grew exponentially, and the art world took notice.

Less than obvious, however, was the start of an Absolut tradition. This was the first example of an Absolut mentor and protégé at work. Haring must have looked at ABSOLUT WARHOL and thought to himself, "That was fine for Andy. But what do I do that's me?" Certainly he wanted Warhol's praise and approval, but the work had to be uniquely his.

ABSOLUT BROMOVA.

· Turn the clock forward seventeen years. (That's some clock!) Daniel Gaujac concocts a new super plan for an Absolut art program. Building on a much earlier idea by our New York curator for the Absolut art collection, Marion Kahan, Absolut would invite the ORIGINALS (and other) artists to select their protégés to create new Absolut art. It could be a collaboration, a competition, a salute to the mentor, or even some interaction yet to be imagined. Most important, the protégé should be a newer, younger, striving artist, part of the next wave or generation to come. Hence, ABSOLUT GENERATIONS was born.

The kicker—and this is some kicker!—was Venice. The results of these collaborations were then exhibited during the summer 2003 Venice Biennale—at the Palazzo Zenobio, a seventeenth-century palace that was originally a college for spiritual teaching. How appropriate.

The Biennale, the first truly international art exhibition, had its first showing in 1904. It's also the longest—staying open for six months—and the biggest—welcoming one million visitors. Every country is invited, each having a pavilion displaying (typically) the work of a single representative artists. It's quite an honor to have one's work on display; for many, it's the culmination of an entire career.

When the Biennale director, Marco Bonami, heard about the latest Absolut collaborations, he invited Absolut to be an official participant. This was pretty startling, since the exhibition had always been limited to independent nations and Absolut, while certainly a state of mind for many, is hardly a country. But a rule change was enacted that also included "others" such as Hong Kong, Wales, and Absolut. Thirteen (established) artists chose sixteen (younger) artists to work with. The younger artists created their Absolut art in advance of Venice. Once there, the pairs were provided with space to work together, and react to one another, while interpreting the "generations" theme.

Not surprisingly, these pairings came up with a few surprises:

ABSOLUT BLUE NOSES How shocking: Two guys wearing blue caps on their noses don't take art too seriously. The Blue Noses (Viacheslav Mizin and Alexander Shaburov) are from Novosibirsk, Siberia and were paired with Oleg Kulik. "The ice-hole photograph will be something we will never forget." Sasha can't swim so he clutched the edge of the ice, refusing to let go, as we photographed him. Mizin went cold crazy and simply forgot to don his swimming trunks, thus increasing the retouching budget.

ABSOLUT BROMOVÁ Veronica Bromová, paired with Jan Saudek, is from the Czech Republic. She called her work

ABSOLUT DELPHINE.

ABSOLUT DJORDJADZE.

ABSOLUT FERNSTRÖM.

BSOLUT HARONI.

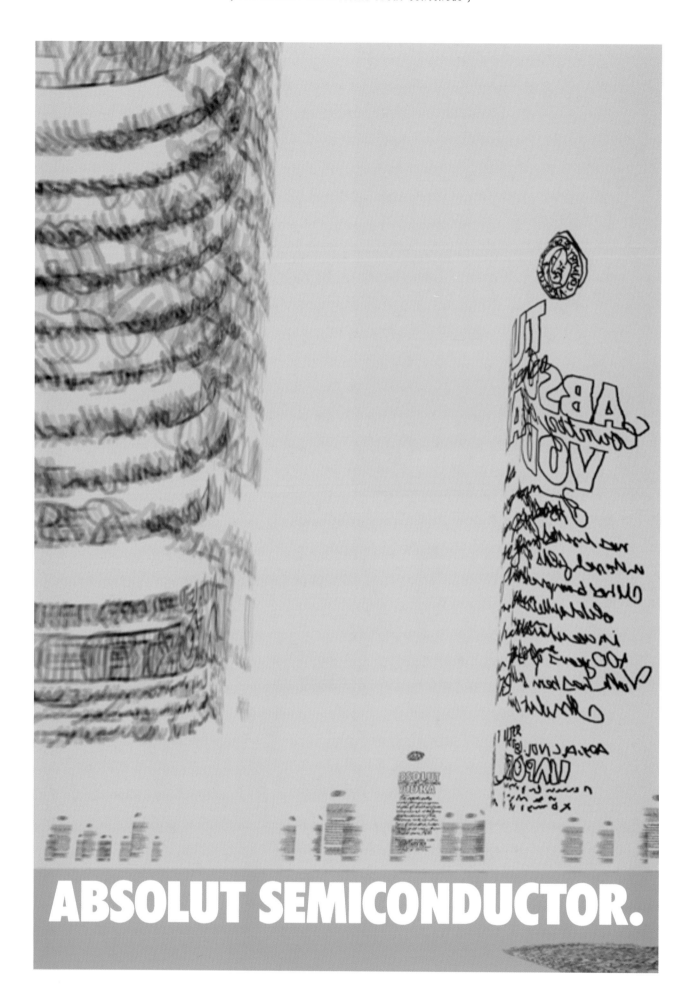

ABSOLUT SEMICONDUCTOR.

ABSOLUT MERCIER.

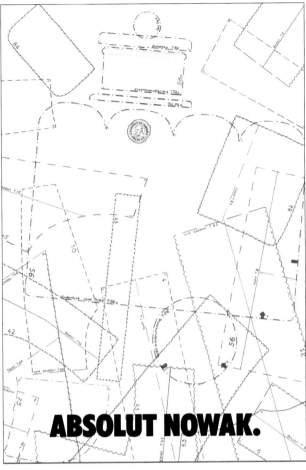

ABSOLUT NOWAK.

ABSOLUT ME—as it represents her swimming. She portrays a human bridge, carrying two lit Absolut bottles, one red, one yellow. "It doesn't particularly mean anything, but it's like the atmosphere of the universe, let's say…. In the end, everything has for me the same value, whether it's Absolut, or the human body, or a carpet. Everything is a thing, and the world is made up of lots of things."

ABSOLUT CUSSOL Beatricé Cussol, who was paired with the artist known as Ben, is from Toulouse, France. A writer and a painter, Cussol creates paintings that tell stories. Here, she realized a bottle love story: "I decided to make two bottles look like a couple joined together. I began by painting one bottle so that when you folded the paper, the second bottle appeared—like one figure giving birth to another."

ABSOLUT DELPHINE Delphine, paired with Wim Delvoye, is from Brussels but lives in London. "I thought the bottle was a little like me." It actually needed a comfortable chair. "It's a kind of pop star, too. It's famous. It's got style. It's glamorous. So I created this enormous, comfortable chair for this beautiful star."

ABSOLUT DJORDJADZE Thea Djordjadze is from Tblisi, Georgia and lives in Germany. She was paired with Rosemarie Trockel. "My current fascination is with the space of mirrors. For Absolut, I used the cut-outs as stencils for sandblasting the mirror-bottle. I created an object that both reflects images and is translucent."

ABSOLUT FERNSTRÖM Linn Fernström, paired with Dan Wolgers, was born in Orebo, Sweden and lives in Stockholm. "My first thought was to make a work of art that is more than an advertising gimmick. [Bravo!] I had three components: myself, the name of the project, and the bottle itself. And then I thought, 'I'll kill you.' The composition emerged out of these ideas: a self-portrait where I am holding Dan Wolgers' head under one arm and the vodka bottle under the other."

ABSOLUT HARONITAKI Aspassio Haronitaki was born in Greece and lives in Paris. Imagine his surprise when he was paired with Louise Bourgeois, the American sculptor well into her tenth decade. Haronitaki explores the relationship between human and animal characteristics and is particularly fascinated by the zebra: "It's a peaceful animal…it represents liberty." Meanwhile, Bourgeois saw ABSOLUT GENERATIONS as an echo of her art school days in Paris, where she 'lived with' the statue of Oedipus. She created ABSOLUT SPIDER out of jam, iron thread, and aluminum foil. And, of course, the bottle.

ABSOLUT SEMICONDUCTOR Semiconductor is the music,

ABSOLUT POUSTTCHI.

ABSOLUT PREGO.

ABSOLUT RENNER.

ABSOLUT SALVINO.

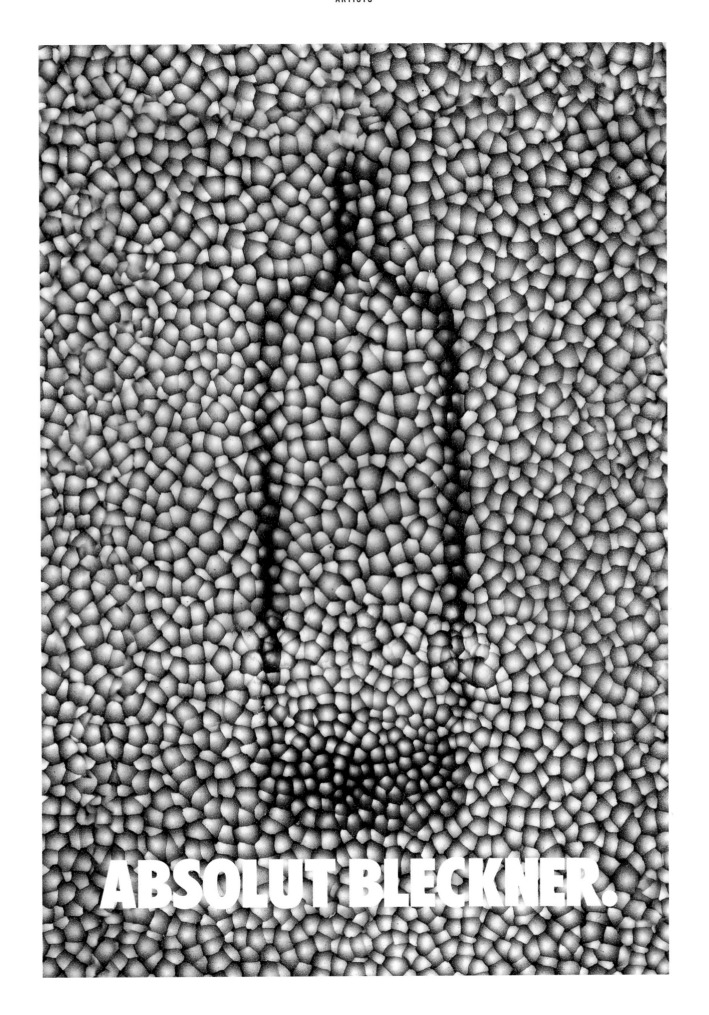

sound, and film duo Ruth Jarman and Joseph Gerhardt from Brighton, England. They were paired with Richard Wentworth. This image is a still from the film they created, a virtual landscape of bottles that look like buildings.

ABSOLUT MERCIER Matthier Mercier was born in Conflans-Saint-Honorie, France, and lives in Paris. He was paired with Olivier Gagnère. Mercier often uses lamps in his work. "Lights are very symbolic, especially in a religious context. The Statue of Liberty is holding a light, representing freedom and knowledge."

ABSOLUT NOWAK Marzena Nowak, paired with Miroslaw Balka, is from Piaseczno, Poland. As a child she observed her mother sewing clothes from magazine patterns. In Nowak's work these cut-outs have become constellations of stars. Or sew-your-own Absolut bottles.

ABSOLUT POUSTTCHI Paired with Rosemarie Trockel, Bettina Pousttchi is from Mainz, Germany. Pousttchi has brought the character and personal world of Katharina, a lip-syncher and dancer, to life—frolicking between the red and white brushes of her parents' car wash. (If you read that sentence twice it will make more sense to you….)

ABSOLUT PREGO Sergio Prego was born in San Sebastian, Spain, and lives in New York. He was paired with Miquel Barceló. Prego decided to make a party instead of a painting. He created a party space with hidden cameras that were triggered by the arriving partygoers or upon opening the refrigerator to fetch a drink. ABSOLUT PREGO is the collage of that evening. Some people thought it was shot in Sing Sing. It wasn't.

ABSOLUT RENNER Lois Renner is from Salzburg, Austria, and was paired with Hans Hollein. He plays with our sense of scale. Placing an actual-size bottle of Absolut in a small-sized room, he turns the bottle into a pop star. "The room regains size by virtue of the things it encloses." Get it?

ABSOLUT SALVINO Andrea Salvino, paired with Enzo Cucchi, was born in Rome. Salvino's work is inspired by the news: stories with a political and social dimension. ABSOLUT SALVINO is a landscape which has been burned by human beings. "It's about decadence and about a willingness to tell the other side of history."

Curating the Absolut exhibition was a real challenge. Remember, each traditional pavilion represented just one country. But Paolo Tognon and Hervé Landry had to arrange thirty-nine artworks representing thirteen countries. The city of Venice was so impressed by the outcome that it invited Absolut to create the ad publicizing the exhibition. (Think about this twist: Absolut's role had always been the "commissioner" of art. Now it had received a "commission.") The result is ABSOLUT BIENNALE by Thomas Grünfeld. The Opening Night was a huge success, attracting 5,000 guests in the sultry Venice heat. And so, the march of time continues: it won't be too long before today's protégés are tomorrow's mentors.

Meanwhile, back in the USA, two new significant artists—Ross Bleckner and Nam Jun Paik—contributed to the campaign.

ABSOLUT BLECKNER You have to give Ross Bleckner credit: he didn't oversubscribe to getting the bottle shape down perfectly. Chalk one up for artistic license. I also remember that Carl Horton was especially fond of what he called the "pebbles ad."

ABSOLUT PAIK Since you can't plug in the ABSOLUT PAIK structure shown on this page, it's impossible to appreciate the majesty and complexity of the piece. Look closely and you can see the wires searching for enough power to keep Paik cooking without blowing another circuit breaker. Paik's combination of Absolut video, music, neon, and tubing are a testament to Paik's forty-year commitment to video as an art form. Korean born, Paik was another member of the Fluxus art movement. What better way to bring Absolut into the twenty-first century than with the grandfather of the video art movement, combining his visions to test the boundaries of Absolut, the bottle and the presentation of art as installation, as entertainment, as flashing lights.

Is it so farfetched to imagine art students, a generation from now, studying Absolut ART 101, and its impact on the "real" art world?

ABSOLUT PAIK.

ABSOLUT ISTVAN

ISTVAN BANYAI IS AN INGENIOUS HUNGARIAN ILLUSTRATOR AND AUTHOR of several books. He did a series titled ZOOM! In it, the camera keeps pulling back from a scene to reveal an entirely different perspective. At the urging of then *New York* magazine editor Kurt Andersen, Banyai created a minibook, ABSOLUT ZOOM, that was bound into an issue of *New York*. It is reproduced here.

ARS that sign had
iled to the old
e center of town,
a junk yard cAn
a broken down
ch his head and

tification Comittee.
red the old man's
public haZard. It
business, bUt an
ave people a pOor
f the toWn. Even
gn maDe NO seNse.
e original lettering,
nly one word was
eft: ABSOLUT.

With the committee
one, Mr. Purvis
oamEd dazedly
hrough the lot.
Useless! UsEless,
enseLess junk," he
uttered, dragging
ipes AND storm window
rames and sinks into
heAp to clear the
dges of his property.
o keep the rickety
ile frOm shifting,
r. Purvis lashed it
ll together with metal
ire. Its silvery glow
l the sun|ight ©ould
be seen
or miles around. At first
from ladders, then from
last piece in place was a
length of aluminum pipe.
e towering conglomeration
tructure in town.
re mYstified. They
down as they drove by.
aper ran a picture of
hoisting his sign on to

the front of the thing. Artists se
easels and painted the evoca
configuration. Surely it represe
the harnessed power and fierce be
of modern technology. Wa
woman? men wondered. Obvi
a man, wOmen thought. Pa
brought their children who k
right away it was a bottle.
fLew low ov
Tourists
their way to the massiv
A television nEws team
night Mr. Purvis's weat
filled screens all over t
as the inTerviewer aske
buiLt this strange creAt
"Well, now, I'm not r
he said, scratching his he
I'm just trYing to do
always done, give people
they need, but don't e
they want."
"And what would tha
puzzled interviewer
"That," Mr. Purv
pointing up
with i

ABS

McGARRY

WRITERS

chapter three

I HAVE ALWAYS BEEN A VORACIOUS READER. NEWSPAPERS, MAGAZINES, CEREAL BOXES, books, even my neighbor's mail: if they happen to leave it out in the open. It's not that I'm snoopy. I just like to keep my eyes open and my mind busy. I rarely leave home without something to read, usually the *New York Times*, so I can occupy myself when I'm in line at the post office or the deli counter at the supermarket. While the other customers are getting restless, I'm checking out the temperatures in the European capitals; scrutinizing the baseball standings for mid-season surprises; trying to maintain a political and pun balance by reading Bill Safire. So much to know. So much to find out.

But books are my real reading passion. I don't keep one handcuffed to my wrist when I'm on line at Citibank—I'm not very good at the two-minute read. Books deserve—and require—my full attention. That's me. There's a commuter on my morning train into New York City who, when we arrive at Grand Central Station, disembarks, but continues reading on the platform as everyone else rushes by. And I don't mean he's finishing sentences, paragraphs, or pages. He's finishing chapters! I've watched. He's there for minutes. I'm so jealous.

As has surely become evident, we're always on the prowl for new creative paths for Absolut. Back in 1997, we were sniffing around, looking for that next door to open. We had been famously successful with artists, fashion designers, composers, even a short foray with a few architects. (I think we even considered asking accountants to do ads.) Anyway, it was the creative director at the time, Eric McClellan, who had the idea for a "writers" series.

Eric had recently been promoted to creative director at TBWA\Chiat\Day. He was very young and self-confident, right out of the Chiat/Day mold. He was a big, loud, threatening, stick-his-chest-in-your-face kind of guy. But he also had this genteel, raised-in-Mississippi side, and could turn on the Southern charm if it suited his purpose. During one of our internal brainstorming sessions, he suggested we commission real authors to write original Absolut stories. The only requirement would be a mention of Absolut within the story. What an obviously good idea. And since the Absolut "bottle" would be a word and not a graphic representation, we would forgo the usual bottle treatment. Meaning: no bottle.

As you would expect, I loved the idea. But I wondered how many different ways could anyone write about Absolut? I could think of only three possibilities: pouring and consuming a drink, playing the adolescent kissing game "spin the bottle" and, finally, hitting someone over the head with the bottle. Could it actually be that limiting?

And where would we begin? Since I was the only member of the team who actually read books—obviously I'm exaggerating—I was nominated to choose the authors we would approach.

I knew we would have to begin with well-known writers. They wouldn't have to be Warhol-famous—but they should be recognizable to readers of the *New Yorker*, *Vanity Fair*, *Harper's*, and the like. Alert readers would know from the ad's headline, lots of copy, and lack of the omnipresent Absolut bottle that this was a different Absolut ad. A different Absolut series. But the writers shouldn't be too well known: We

wouldn't invite John Grisham, Jackie Collins, or Stephen King. Not because we're too "highbrow," we're not. But because of their popularity, they wouldn't be "special" enough. Just well-known and probably expensive.

We decided this shouldn't be a "Discover Unknown Absolut Writers Series" either. That felt too academic, too "We're the teacher, you're the student." Rather, these should be writers who represented a certain degree of Absolut creativity. Taken as a group, they would make up an interesting little library for Thursday night book discussions. They should be successful, but not too rich. Oh, and they should be writers I like to read.

ABSOLUT DUNNE So why did we open with Dominick Dunne? Probably because he defied easy categorization. Dunne, a novelist, screenwriter, and journalist, has been writing since the 1940s, from his days in Hollywood. I had been reading his pieces in *Vanity Fair* for several years, especially the riveting updates from the O. J. Simpson trial. He's been a chronicler of the rich, the corrupt, and the criminal for decades. Yet underneath all that muckraking, he's actually a sweet guy and a survivor. And he gave us a fast yes. One more "and"—Dunne is an ex-drinker, but we assured him that was irrelevant. In **ABSOLUT DUNNE**, the Absolut bottle is a rain-soaked gift to "Bill Slocum's" ex-wife, Sophie Fairfax, a Broadway actress he's visiting in her dressing room. Look closely at the theater poster and you'll see the art directors' Hitchcockian touch: (Dan) Braun and (Bart) Slomkowski appear as producers.

The first ad went off without a hitch. Dunne gave a reading at Patroon, a macho steakhouse in NYC. Nobody was embarrassed to be there. Dunne's agent, Owen Laster, seemed pleased that the Absolut connection was a positive one for his client. The press even noticed. The *New York Post's* "Page 6," their gossip sheet, called it an "Absolut Coup."

We were off to the races. Of course, not every writer we contacted wanted to write for Absolut. It fell to Kitty Hall, our classy Southern belle/account supervisor from Charlotte, N.C., to contact the agents and convince them this was a great idea. Then she had to convince us that a particular writer was the right choice. I remember she received a hand-typed note from John Updike graciously declining. The note was good enough to publish. But Kitty hammered away and soon we had our very own literary salon.

ABSOLUT IRVING If I have to tell you who John Irving is, don't tell me. Spare yourself the shame. Irving jumped into the assignment with great enthusiasm, mentioning Absolut frequently. Actually, the story revolves around a daily tryst in Aspen's Hotel Jerome, where our unnamed but laid-up hero gets to sip Absolut from a woman's bellybutton, as it "was as deep as a well." I do recall one episode of editorial excitement by the client. Bob Bernstein, a very affable and dawn-to-dusk-at-the-desk guy, had a problem with how the protagonist gets injured: a shot glass breaks in a hot tub; he steps on it creating a nasty cut. "Don't you know we have a policy at Seagram against drinking in hot tubs?" Bernstein asked steamily. We do now. And John Irving didn't miss a beat. He moved the mishap to the shower. Where, oddly, we didn't hear a peep about policy.

ABSOLUT ALVAREZ Julia Alvarez, as Kitty Hall informed me, is an exciting writer from the Dominican Republic. As we hadn't yet introduced a female writer, it was already about time. Alvarez is the author of *How the Garcia Girls Lost Their Accents* and *In the Time of the Butterflies.* ABSOLUT ALVAREZ is her lighthearted and fictionalized story of a slightly crazy priest, and it created a bit of a stir. She—and Absolut—were accused by the Catholic League of trivializing the communion Host by referring to it as "everybody's least favorite Easter candy." Alvarez explained that the Easter candy was just that: candy put into the ciborium by a priest who was a little nutty. Rather than asking Alvarez to rewrite the offending section, we pulled the ad to keep the peace, which didn't make anyone happy except the Catholic League. This was another example—a rare one for Absolut—where art, tangling with religion, with business in the middle, sometimes has to fold.

ABSOLUT GOLDEN Like so many people, when I read Arthur Golden's *Memoirs of a Geisha*, it revealed a world that I not only knew absolutely nothing about, but one that I didn't know could be so fascinating. Coincidentally, the accompanying artwork—by Polly Becker—of a geisha marionette looks like a dancing Absolut bottle. Golden spent several years working on this novel while teaching English to Japanese children. I met him at a charity event Absolut sponsored, "Seconding the First," an evening of entertainment supporting the First Amendment. He told me, seriously, I think, that his friends had told him that he had finally made it; he'd done an Absolut ad. We thought so, too.

ABSOLUT COUPLAND Like it or not, Doug Coupland is irreversibly linked with "Generation X," the title of his first novel that was the cultural angst-ray for the Yuppies' kid brothers and sisters (aka slackers). Voices of a generation typically are drafted (as opposed to volunteering): "I speak for myself, not for a generation. I never have." But this Canadian author and artist brought a certain 1990s edginess to his work as a nervous futurist that both critics and Xers were drawn to. For Absolut, Coupland writes of a "mountain" climb in Los Angeles "maybe because there will be wisdom up at the top." No one seems to remember why we have two(!) Absolut bottles in the illustrations. Were we losing our nerve?

ABSOLUT BOYLE T. C. (Thomas Coraghessan) Boyle was another favorite of Kitty Hall. "C'mon, Richard, he's good. Really good." This was becoming fun. People were reminding me that I didn't know everything and the clients started reading the authors' books, too. Lars Nellmer, the veep of marketing at Absolut in Stockholm, became a full-fledged member of this new book "club." Lars may have been short in stature, as he'd frequently remind you in self-jest, but he was never short in the intuition department: "I'm not sure if the Absolut consumers like this writers' series but I know I do. Let's do some more."

The narrator of Boyle's story is a writer on retreat with his wife, working on a biography of John Muir (the naturalist who founded the Sierra Club). He's reminded about Nature's duality—beauty and danger—as he goes off on a simple walk through the woods.

ABSOLUT JUNGER I got caught up in *The Perfect Storm*, Sebastian Junger's breakthrough book, and passed it around to all my friends. The story of the sad, doomed sword-fishermen aboard the Andrea Gail was riveting. Junger, author, journalist, and adventurer, has made a career of writing from dangerous climes. My first reading of ABSOLUT JUNGER had me sure the bottle was going to be cracked over someone's head. Phew.

ABSOLUT McGARRY MORRIS I really liked this story of Purvis the junk-man, an eBay man before his time. I also appreciated the author's insistence of headlining the work McGARRY MORRIS. It certainly prevented Morris-confusion with authors of the same name. I remember we paid a type designer a lot of money to make the copy extra difficult to read. (I'm very old-fashioned. I want the readers to be able to READ the stories.) And McGarry Morris's Absolut sculpture tower was pretty cool.

ABSOLUT CHEVALIER *Girl with a Pearl Earring* is one of those magical, transporting "little" books that spirits you out of the fin de siecle—the twentieth in this case—and right, smack dab into Holland in the seventeenth. Tracy Chevalier—even her name is romantic—wrote *Pearl* while she was pregnant with her son, finishing just before he was born. I bet none of us will ever again look at Johannes Vermeer's mysterious painting, the inspiration for the book,

There was a summer storm. Lightning. Thunder. Pelting rain.

William Slocum, known as Will to his friends, made his way down the alleyway by the side of the theater until he arrived at the stage door. In one hand he held a broken umbrella over his head and in the other he clutched a shopping bag to him, protectively.

"I'm soaked," said Will, coming inside and shaking the water off him.

Danny, who managed the stage door, put up his hands to stop Will from coming any further inside.

"Close your umbrella outside, not in here, fella. Don't drip anywhere."

"Sorry about that," said Will. "May I put this package down on your table for a minute? The bottom's come through in the rain, and I just rescued this gift in time, or it would have smashed to pieces in that damn alleyway. I'm here to see Miss Fairfax."

ABSOLUT

"Is she expecting you?" Danny picked up his list and perused it. "Miss Fairfax didn't tell me she was expecting any visitors."

"She's not expecting me. It's a surprise," said Will.

"Does she know you?"

"Oh, yes. We used to be married."

"Name?"

"William Slocum, but it will spoil the surprise."

"Okay, okay," said Danny, having sized him up: Good suit. Good shirt. Good shoes. "Go on up. Dressing room #8 on the second floor. Here, don't forget your package."

Sophie Fairfax was sitting at her dressing table, applying cold cream over her theatrical makeup, when there was a knock at her door. "You can't come in yet, whoever it is," she called out. Then she added, "Who is it?"

"Me," said Will, opening the door.

"Oh, for God's sake, Will, what the hell are you doing here?" she asked. "How did you get by Danny at the stage door? He's supposed to keep people like you out."

"I told him we used to be married," said Will.

"You're the only 42-year-old man I know who still acts like an undergraduate prankster. I told you when I left you that the act was getting tired," said Sophie, rubbing her face with Kleenex. "Did you see the play?"

"Yes."

"No compliments?"

"You were wonderful."

"I'm not supposed to have to beg for that. That should have been your entrance line. What's that bedraggled package you're clasping to your bosom?"

"You may not believe this, Sophie, but I miss you," said Will.

"Enough, enough," replied Sophie.

"You may not believe this either, but when I left my apartment, this bottle of Absolut was beautifully wrapped in silver paper with dark blue ribbons, in honor of your birthday, but I was jostled in the subway, and it dropped on the floor and got kicked, which is why the paper's torn. There was a card, such a funny card, saying "Forgive me" — perfect for the occasion — but it seems to have gotten lost, and then the shopping bag got wet and the bottom came out and it almost dropped again in the alley, and, anyway, Happy Birthday."

"I remember a time when your presents came in little velvet boxes," said Sophie, starting to apply her street makeup.

"When you moved out, you threw a velvet box at me, and I got a black eye," said Will.

"You did not get a black eye," replied Sophie.

"Almost." He placed the bottle on her dressing table. "This seemed more appropriate under the circumstances. I didn't want to be showy."

"I'm mad about the bottle," said Sophie. "Perfect for forsythia."

"How about a nip on a rainy night off Broadway?"

"Oh, why not? Are you planning on taking me out to supper?"

DUNNE.

Snow, even in the city, reminded him of skiing, which he had given up. His wife didn't ski. In his bachelor days, he had associated his ski vacations with romantic encounters. Single girls who skied were not averse to speed, or to other physical risks. He'd once met a Dutch girl in Klosters. She was too tall for the bed at the Chesa Grischuna, where (in the athleticism of their lovemaking) she'd broken her right big toe against the headboard and couldn't ski for the rest of her holiday. He had escaped that relationship with only minor injuries.

He'd suffered more lasting scars from an adventure in Aspen, of which (despite the passage of time) he was enduringly fond. She was a German girl who drank Absolut, straight out of the freezer, while she overheated herself in his shower at the Hotel Jerome. She'd made an unheard-of deal with room service: they brought her the frosted fifth of vodka—a full bottle—and a frozen shot glass. She offered him an icy swallow, but his hand was wet, the shot glass was slippery, and he dropped the small, heavy glass in the steamy shower. He promptly stepped on it, cutting his foot.

Then *he* was the one who couldn't ski. The stitches, in the ball of his left foot, made him limp on his heel. But while the German girl skied, he happily anticipated her daily arrival in his room at the Jerome. She was admirably consistent: she would begin by ordering the frosty bottle, which was always full, and the ice-cold shot glass. He still dreamed about her reddened skin, smelling of the pine-scented soap from the shower. Usually her hair was wet; he couldn't recall its true color.

She was traveling with her parents—and with her kid sister, with whom she shared a room. She had to have dinner with her family every evening. If she ever spent the night with him, her sister would have ratted to her parents, but their late-afternoon liaisons were all that he could have hoped for.

One afternoon, in the passion of the moment, the shot glass rolled under the bed. The German girl proposed that they sip the half-frozen vodka from each other's bellybutton. His navel was disappointingly shallow. In the waning light, as the room grew colder, his bed got wet. As he remembered it, the girl's bellybutton was as deep as a well. He never spilled—he drank every drop.

Now, as the newfallen snow blanketed Manhattan, he remembered the German girl's navel—and her other exciting parts. From the kitchen freezer of his apartment, he poured himself a shot glass of Absolut. He kept the bottle and the shot glass in the rear of the freezer, behind the frozen fish sticks and the frozen peas and corn, the Popsicles that the children liked, and his wife's homemade tomato sauce.

One chilly swallow of the vodka, and the snow that was falling on Lexington Avenue could have been falling on Aspen—dotting the heads and shoulders of the tired skiers returning to the Hotel Jerome.

He never regretted that his wife didn't ski, or that she wore socks to bed and would have slapped him if he'd ever poured half-frozen vodka in her navel. He loved family life. The risks of skiing, and romantic encounters, no longer tempted him. Now, even when it snowed, the Absolut sufficed.

ABSOLUT IRVING.

I went down to the island to do a piece on the uses & misuses of the land and THERE i met some men and women who wanted to keep the rain forest alive, the rivers clear, the stars in the sky. They said, there is a man who says he is a priest who has BEEN talking the farmers into selling to the Canadians. So we went to SEE him at his makeshift chapel and there on the altar was an Absolut bottle full of cayennas and birds of paradise. So I said, where did you get the bottle, thinking of the Canadians at the dam settlement. And he said, My child, all objects on this altar are rELigious articles, the chalice that looked like a wineglass, the oilcloth altarcloth with slices of pink watermelon, the paten like a plate for a spoon with which to stir a concoction, the precious ciborium full of what looked like everybody's least favorite EASTER candy... But what about the bottle, i pointed to the vase of flowers. That is latin for God almIGhty Absolut Absolutorum he said in pig Latin From the pLAYGround, spreadinG his arms as if hAving said the magic words he could now take off into the sky.

ABSOLUT ALVAREZ.

KOHINA TURNED OUT TO BE AN EVEN MORE CELEBRATED GEISHA THAN I WAS IN MY PRIME, but I don't think she ever recognized her own beauty. She never understood why men treated her the way they did. I remember when she was an apprentice, there was a certain actor—let's call him Mr. Ikeda—who used to come to the Gion district all the time. He was quite popular among the geisha because he was rarely moody, but he never once asked for me—until, that is, I took on Kohina as my younger sister and began to train her. I could tell from the start that Kohina found him enchanting: she'd seen all his films, and she was in awe, really. Yet somehow it never occurred to her he might feel attracted to her too.

Then one evening as we arrived at the Mitsuyo Teahouse, the mistress took us aside to say that Mr. Ikeda had been sitting alone a half-hour in the little room overlooking the moss garden, turning down all her offers of company, just waiting for us and no one else. We slid the door open a crack to peek in, and there he sat, drawing lines in the beaded moisture on an unopened bottle of Absolut Vodka. Beside it on the table stood two un-touched glasses. "Only two glasses," I said to Kohina. "He's waiting for you, not both of us."

She was wearing a cinnamon-colored kimono with a design of autumn grasses, and she looked magnificent, but I could see she had no confidence in herself. I'm not sure what she would have done if I hadn't stepped aside and slid the door open so she had no choice but to go in. She gave me such a look! Nervous and excited all at once. The flush in her skin reminded me how she'd appeared that afternoon when she'd stepped from the bath into the chilly air, still steaming.

ABSOLUT GOLDEN.

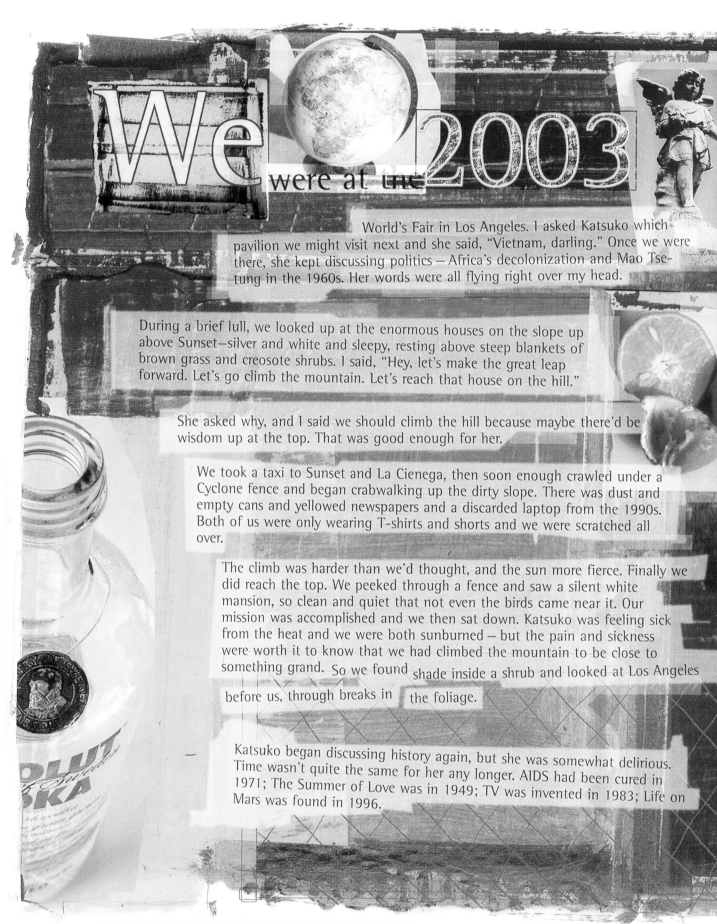

We ⊕ were at the 2003

World's Fair in Los Angeles. I asked Katsuko which pavilion we might visit next and she said, "Vietnam, darling." Once we were there, she kept discussing politics — Africa's decolonization and Mao Tse-tung in the 1960s. Her words were all flying right over my head.

During a brief lull, we looked up at the enormous houses on the slope up above Sunset—silver and white and sleepy, resting above steep blankets of brown grass and creosote shrubs. I said, "Hey, let's make the great leap forward. Let's go climb the mountain. Let's reach that house on the hill."

She asked why, and I said we should climb the hill because maybe there'd be wisdom up at the top. That was good enough for her.

We took a taxi to Sunset and La Cienega, then soon enough crawled under a Cyclone fence and began crabwalking up the dirty slope. There was dust and empty cans and yellowed newspapers and a discarded laptop from the 1990s. Both of us were only wearing T-shirts and shorts and we were scratched all over.

The climb was harder than we'd thought, and the sun more fierce. Finally we did reach the top. We peeked through a fence and saw a silent white mansion, so clean and quiet that not even the birds came near it. Our mission was accomplished and we then sat down. Katsuko was feeling sick from the heat and we were both sunburned — but the pain and sickness were worth it to know that we had climbed the mountain to be close to something grand. So we found shade inside a shrub and looked at Los Angeles before us, through breaks in the foliage.

Katsuko began discussing history again, but she was somewhat delirious. Time wasn't quite the same for her any longer. AIDS had been cured in 1971; The Summer of Love was in 1949; TV was invented in 1983; Life on Mars was found in 1996.

While Katsuko unraveled time I thought about the smells and objects of day as the heat tickled memory cells in my brain. I remembered the fabric softener in the morning's laundry; the scent of the

tangerines we squished into glasses of Absolut at the Vietnamese Pavilion. There was an 18-wheeler that belched smoke at us on the freeway, and there was a dusty, woman's Dynel wig we saw in a thrift shop.

Sometimes a day can seem random. And then five years later you realize the day wasn't random at all. And as for Katsuko as well as myself, time really hasn't felt the same ever since that day we climbed the hill.

end

ABSOLUT COUPLAND.

He swore to himself he'd never leave the cabin without a daypack. This was wild country out here, nearly eight thousand feet up in the Sequoia National Forest, and too many things could go wrong. He pictured that daypack now, the sort of thing that might contain matches, a compass, flashlight, granola bars, a tarp and groundcloth – better yet, a cell phone. It was dusk, temperature in the teens, and there was a mountain – or maybe two mountains – between him and the cabin. Worse: it had begun to snow, a hard piling snow that drew a screen over the visible world. He didn't need a little voice whispering in his ear to know he was lost.

Two hours ago, he'd got up from his desk, shrugged into his parka and wandered off into the woods. He didn't tell anyone he was going (Maggie was on the couch with a book, a very dull book, judging from the sound of her breathing and the weight of her eyelids), and it was no big deal – he'd gone out and followed his feet just about every day since they'd rented the place. It cleared his head. And it brought him close, in spirit at least, to John Muir, the subject of the biography he was working on.

But he was no woodsman, no rapt visionary who would climb up into a tree in the middle of a blizzard just to feel what a tree must feel, and he liked to take nature in comfortably sectioned pieces, an hour or two at a time. What did the snow taste like? Like frozen air, air made concrete, and he let it coat his tongue and drift across his upturned face. He wasn't cold. And he wasn't panicky. Not yet.

Then it was night, night like a succubus, steaming up out of the ground to meld with the pale sky, and still the snow kept coming. He could see nothing. He was breathing hard, slashing through drifts that were knee-deep, going up, going down, going nowhere. People die out here, that's what he was thinking, and he could feel it – death, as palpable as the cold – seeping into his fingers and toes. He thought vaguely of building a shelter, pine boughs, layers of snow, some sort of lean-to, but when he pictured it, in the abstract, it looked too much like a grave.

Later, much later, when he was so sapped he could barely lift his feet, he blundered into something in the dark, something that wasn't the wall-like trunk of a sequoia or ponderosa, but a wall in fact. And as he felt along the wall, he came to a door, and the door opened to his touch. A moment later, he was in front of the fire, the embers there, a handful of kindling, another log, and the light quavered and rose and he saw Maggie stretched out on the couch, in the moment of waking, the book collapsed like a big insect on her chest. "Hey," she said, "you're all snow. Been out for a walk?"

"Something like that," he said, and it was as if he were the one who'd been asleep and dreaming. "But listen," and he was already moving away from the fire, the familiar bottle in his hand, the two glasses, a squeeze of lime, the rejuvenant smell of the Absolut, "how about a drink before dinner? To celebrate."

ABSOLUT BOYLE.

The trouble started when one of the Moroccans grabbed Claudio's Viking helmet. It was plastic with fake rubies along the rim and two horns on top, and the Moroccan shouted that it had been stolen from him the night before and what kind of swine would steal a man's helmet. It was festival time and Claudio was in a t-shirt and shorts with a leather wineskin over his shoulder. He spun around and got a grip on the plastic rim and two of his friends jumped in and then another Spaniard with nothing better to do got his hand on it. The other patrons made room for whatever problem was coming and the five men stood glaring at each other in the middle of the sawdust floor with the helmet gripped between them.

T-shirt

ABSOLUT VODKA

"Idiotas," the second Spaniard's girlfriend muttered, and walked out. The men started pulling again.

Staggering around the room like a ten-legged animal while the bartender slowly moved out from behind the bar with a bottle gripped in one hand. The men crashed into a table and then into the crowd and Claudio yelled,

Para! Para! Para!

because the helmet had started to rip along its plastic seam. The men were about to destroy the very thing they wanted, and every one waited to see what they would do. "Se esta rompiendo," Claudio said quietly. The first Moroccan nodded but did not offer to let go. No one did. Claudio looked around until he found my face in the crowd and motioned me over. I worked my way to where he stood and asked him what he wanted. "Will you hold this helmet as I would?" he asked. "Yes," I said. "Will you defend it as if it were your own?" I nodded. Claudio placed my hand on the rim and then went over to the bartender, who was still standing there with the bottle. "What is the mark?" he asked. "ABSOLUT," the bartender said. "Is that a good one?" "Very good." Claudio lifted the bottle out of the bartender's hand and shouldered his way back through the crowd. The Moroccan looked on suspiciously. Claudio twisted the top open and upended the bottle until the helmet was full. "DEJENLO," Claudio said, holding the helmet from underneath. The rest of us let go and Claudio presented the helmet to the Moroccan, who brought the rim to his mouth and took a respectful swallow. He passed it to his left and the next Moroccan drank and then the other Spaniard drank and finally the last Moroccan took his turn. He gave the helmet to Claudio, who received it like a chalice and knocked a sip back from the rim. From there the helmet went to the bartender, who took a swallow and sent it off around the room. "AHORA?" he said loudly. Claudio gestured at the Moroccans and then slapped his wallet down on the bar. "These men are now my friends," he said. "They are not to pay for another thing."

ABSOLUT JUNGER

without thinking of Chevalier's story. The author used the same magic dust in writing ABSOLUT CHEVALIER. And her device to bring Absolut into the story was natural and unassuming. Just like Absolut itself.

ABSOLUT FURST I've always been a spy guy: you know, the espionage thrillers by writers such as John le Carré, Eric Ambler, Robert Harris, Joseph Kanon, and Robert Wilson. These writers create intelligent, layered, atmospheric thrillers, where Good vs. Evil is filled with gray splotches. Another of these writers I "discovered" several years ago is Alan Furst. He's written ten books, almost quietly, until the publication a few years ago of *Blood of Victory*. I had read his "Paris series": *The World at Night* and *Red Gold,* which take place before and during WWII, and wondered, "why isn't he famous?" (I'm sure he wondered, too.)

What's apparent in **ABSOLUT FURST**—titled "Chapter VII: The Defector"—is his ability to set a scene, draw the characters, create some tension, and resolve it, all in fewer than 200 words. This ad was probably our best marriage of art and copy: credit art director Bill Montgomery, my humble, quiet friend, for selecting Dado Moriyama's roiling seas photograph; along with the Underwood typewriter American typeface, especially the letters filled in from years of pounding out great little stories.

ABSOLUT E. LYNN To some extent, Absolut's Carl Horton napped during the writer's series. Which is to say, he didn't hate it, so he let it continue. Carl really wanted to get Tom Clancy; and while we didn't think Clancy was right for the series, we capitulated since Carl was being so unusually nice about everything. [Un]fortunately, Clancy didn't see it our way and declined. But Carl had another suggestion: E. Lynn Harris. While Carl wasn't a Harris reader, he said all his girlfriends were, which was good enough for us. This began a year-long relationship between Account Director Marilyn Kirk and E. Lynn. ("Please, call me Lynn.") Marilyn, a MENSA member (she told me when I hired her), wisely responded, "Please, call me Marilyn." Harris was so excited about writing for Absolut he just kept on writing and writing and writing. Given the format of the series—250–750 words fit nicely on the page—we had to

KITTY HALL, AFTER HEARING ONE OF MY JOKES.

go back a few times to bring it to our publishable length. Not to mention the dozen different layouts we kept playing with. I think Harris wrote three books while we tinkered with his ad. But finally, we had our gem. And Carl Horton reported that his "women approved it." Amen.

I don't know if we can characterize the writers' series as a great success. I don't know how much Absolut vodka each ad sold, but we never do. I do know it was a sound idea, that we did our little bit to encourage people to read more books by introducing them to interesting authors. And it got all of us at TBWA and Absolut talking about books, even before Oprah and Amazon made it fashionable—and worthwhile—to read again. So, in stretching the campaign's boundaries, we may have even performed a public service.

I remember it clearly.

We were standing by the canal that ran past our families' houses. When we were children we had shared that water. I would throw a stick into the canal that Anton would fish out when it floated by his house. He would use the stick to poke down into the mirrored sky and break up the reflection.

Will you do it? he said. *Will you marry me and find a new canal to live by? The next canal over is rather nice.*

I had never liked the way he used *rather* to dilute what he said.

A bottle was bobbing up and down in the water. In my head I scolded the person who had thrown it in. Brewers made beer from this water. We drank that beer. It was our duty to keep the canals clean.

I wanted to reach down for the bottle but a barge was approaching, loaded with vegetables — cabbages and carrots and potatoes. The barge man leered at me, even with Anton standing at my side. I turned red and tugged the corners of my cap to hide my face.

When the barge had passed I looked again for the bottle. It had disappeared under the churning water.

Anton caught my hands. His own were dry as leaves. *Will you marry me, Anneka? Will you?*

That was another thing I didn't like about him — he repeated words as if I were deaf.

The bottle popped up to the surface, rolling over and over in the wake of the barge. Letters were etched on it. I stepped forward to see.

Will you?

Absolu— I read aloud.

Before I could finish Anton had covered my mouth with his.

And that is how I married your father. Romantic, isn't it?

ABSOLUT CHEVALIER.

FOR 55 YEARS that sign had been nailed to the old fence. Because the junk yard was right in the center of town, Mr. Purvis tried to keep the place as neat as a junk yard can be. If all a person needed was a clutch for a broken down washing machine, Mr. Purvis would scratch his head and move slowly through the lot, even though he knew exactly where to find it. The trick was to give customers plenty of time to browse through the piles. That way they left with things they hadn't even known they needed: a busted window fan, a claw-footed bath tub, dented tin pails. It was an art, Mr. Purvis thought, to take what one person didn't want and match it up with someone who did.

But as the years passed, time was money and people couldn't afford to spend much of either tinkering with balky lawnmowers or sludgy oil burners. Sales dwindled, but Mr. Purvis continued to haul in junk. His rusting piles grew higher and wider. Sometimes now, a week went by without a single sale. Sometimes, two weeks. Under the weight of so much junk, the decrepit fence sagged out over the sidewalk. The sign fell into the weeds, and a passerby propped it against the fence. One day Mr. Purvis's spirits soared as a crowd bustled through the gate. They were from the Downtown Beautification Comittee. They declared the old man's pro®ty a public hazard. It wasn't a valid business, but an eyesore. It gave people a poor impres$ion of the town. Even his peeling sign made NO seNse.

Of the original lettering, only one word was left: ABSOLUT.

With the committee gone, Mr. Purvis roamed dazedly through the lot. "Useless! Useless, senseless junk," he muttered, dragging pipes and storm window frames and sinks into a heap to clear the edges of his property. To keep the rickety pile from shifting, Mr. Purvis lashed it all together with metal wire. Its silvery glow in the sunlight could be seen for miles around. At first he worked from ladders, then from staging. The last piece in place was a thirty-foot length of aluminum pipe. That made the towering conglomeration the tallest structure in town. People were mystified. They slowed way down as they drove by. The newspaper ran a picture of Mr. Purvis hoisting his sign on to

M. Purvis— Purveyor of absolutely everything

the front of the thing. Artists set up easels and painted the evocative configuration. Surely it represented the harnessed power and fierce beauty of modern technology. Was it a woman? men wondered. Obviously a man, women thought. Parents brought their children who knew right away it was a bottle. Planes flew low overhead. Tourists found their way to the massive sculpture. A television news team came. That night Mr. Purvis's weathered face filled screens all over the country as the interviewer asked why he'd built this strange creation. "Well, now, I'm not really sure," he said, scratching his head. "Maybe I'm just trying to do what I've always done, give people something they need, but don't even know they want." "And what would that be?" the puzzled interviewer asked. "That," Mr. Purvis replied, pointing up to the sign with its one legible word.

ABSOLUT McGARRY MORRIS

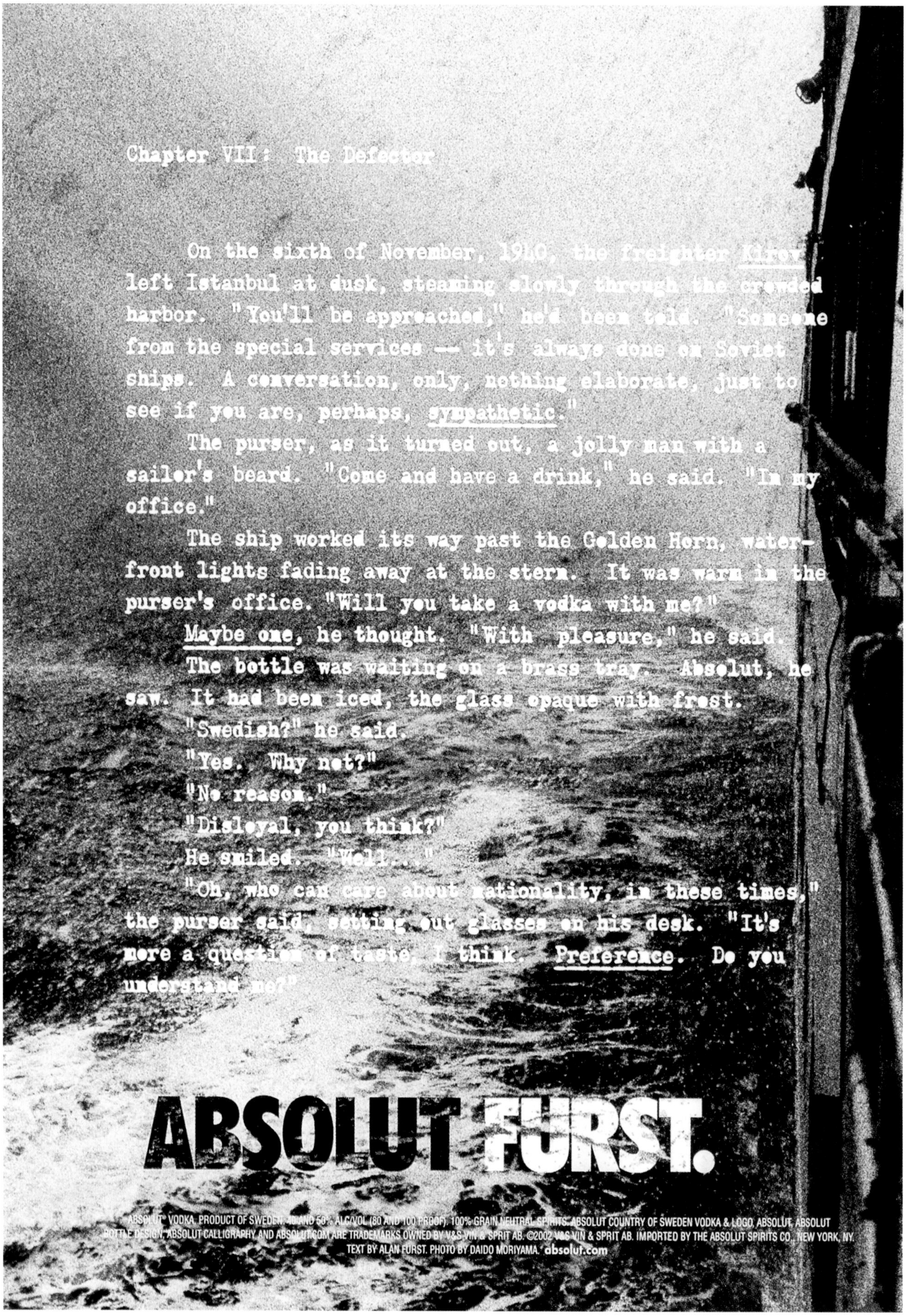

Chapter VII: The Defector

On the sixth of November, 1940, the freighter Kirov left Istanbul at dusk, steaming slowly through the crowded harbor. "You'll be approached," he'd been told. "Someone from the special services — it's always done on Soviet ships. A conversation, only, nothing elaborate, just to see if you are, perhaps, sympathetic."

The purser, as it turned out, a jolly man with a sailor's beard. "Come and have a drink," he said. "In my office."

The ship worked its way past the Golden Horn, water-front lights fading away at the stern. It was warm in the purser's office. "Will you take a vodka with me?"

Maybe one, he thought. "With pleasure," he said.

The bottle was waiting on a brass tray. Absolut, he saw. It had been iced, the glass opaque with frost.

"Swedish?" he said.

"Yes. Why not?"

"No reason."

"Disloyal, you think?"

He smiled. "Well..."

"Oh, who can care about nationality, in these times," the purser said, setting out glasses on his desk. "It's more a question of taste, I think. Preference. Do you understand me?"

ABSOLUT FURST.

I nervously walked into the dimly lit bar.

Our eyes met immediately. Suddenly my head was spinning and my legs were suddenly filled with cement. He smiled and raised an eyebrow suggestively as I moved slowly toward the bar. Moments later I was so close I could feel his warm breath on my face.

"I didn't think you'd come," Bale said.

"You said it was important," I replied as I glanced and admired the quiet sophistication of the small cocktail lounge.

There was a polished oak bar, and lemon-colored light hovered over dozens of different liquor bottles against a mirrored wall. I glanced briefly into his steady brown eyes and then back at the bottles. I knew that if I gazed into his eyes long enough the wonderful, all-enveloping lust, I mean — love would return.

I focused on a thick frosted bottle with a thin neck and bold royal-blue lettering. I gazed at the small black script lettering below and pretended I was reading an important declaration instead of looking at Bale out of the corner of my eye and recalling the miserable evening three years before when he had confessed that my suspicions were correct and he was moving back in with his college fiancée, Nola. The same woman whom he'd promised me he was finished with the first time we made love.

I knew if I looked into his smooth cinnamon brown face I would be in trouble. But for how long? An evening? Week? Month? Maybe even another year.

"Can I get you a drink?" Bale asked as he took a sip from his cocktail glass brimming with a lime and several ice cubes.

"Sure," I said as I caught the eye of the handsome bartender and mouthed, "Dry martini with Absolut please."

"So have you been thinking about me?" Bale asked.

I didn't answer as I watched the bartender pluck the bottle I'd focused on a minute ago. He dramatically poured the clear liquid into a sexy martini glass. After an uncomfortable silence Bale repeated his question.

"What do you mean have I been thinking about you?" I demanded.

"Yo, hold up. I see some things haven't changed. You still have that same edge about you."

"What do you want, Bale? What's so important that you had to see me tonight?" The bartender placed my drink in front of me and I picked it up quickly and took a sip to calm my nerves before I began to tell Bale how many sleepless nights I'd had thinking of nothing but him.

Several moments passed and Bale said, "What would you say if I told you I woke up a couple of mornings ago and realized that I was still in love with you?" He lazily took a drag from a cigarette.

"Is this the truth or is this like the love you offered before?" I asked.

"Don't you remember what I told you before I left?"

"I blocked it out," I lied.

"Baby, truth, like love, is never absolute."

ABSOLUT E. LYNN.

ABSOLUT BETWEEN THE COVERS

I HAD TO CHUCKLE WHEN ONE OF MY FAVORITE WRITERS, JOHN LE CARRE, published *Absolute Friends* in 2004. I thought it so fitting that he, too, couldn't avoid the "word," and even employed the two-word headline. It got me to thinking of the many sightings of Absolut/e in book titles. (After spending nearly two decades breathing Absolut air, this is not unusual.) See, besides the English language where absolute "carries" the e, some languages don't (German); some substitute o for e to create absoluto (Spanish, Italian); Hang on, this gets a little more interesting. It also occurred to me that as Absolut, the vodka, has sunk its jaws into popular culture, popular culture has also consumed Absolut.

If you take a not-so-quick trip through Amazon.com, you'll discover 1,200+ references to Absolut, and most of them are about the vodka. I have filtered out any marketing and business books that blah-blah-blah about the advertising campaign, the how-to-stock-your-bar-and-slather-your-ribs books, and the absolutism theories of Martin Heidegger. (You're welcome.)

What remains, largely, are lots of novels where characters are consuming the vodka, admiring the bottle, and sharing a moment. While this isn't a recommended reading list, by any means, it makes for an interesting tour. Herewith, a short list:

Gone for Good *by Harlen Coben*

Lucky *by Alice Sebold*

The Devil Wears Prada *by Lauren Weisenberger*

Couldn't Keep It to Myself *by Wally Lamb*

The Sweet Potato Queens' Book of Love *by Jill Conner Browne*

Dry *by Augusten Burroughs*

American Psycho *by Brett Easton Ellis*

The Princess Diaries (Volume 2) *by Meg Cabot*

Prayers for Rain *by Dennis LeHane*

The World's Most Dangerous Places *by Robert Young Pelton*

The Sinner *by Tess Gerrittsen*

Insomnia *by Stephen King*

In These Girls, Hope is a Muscle *by Madeline Blais*

The Last Days *by Joel Rosenberg*

Sick Puppy *by Carl Hiassen*

Cold Paradise *by Stuart Woods*

Pandora's Curse *by Jack DuBrul*

Frommer's South Florida *by Lesley Abrovanel*

Dead Irish *by John Lescroart*

OUTSIDE

chapter four

ABSOLUT'S MAGAZINE ADVERTISING CAMPAIGN IS OBVIOUSLY WELL KNOWN. Yet, since the very beginning it has also been a breakthrough brand in advertising outdoors. Because the outdoor advertising landscape is often associated with ugly, interruptive billboards, we decided to take the high road right from the start. During the 1960s there was a bill in Congress called the Highway Beautification Act that was meant to eradicate "advertising blight" on the interstate highway system. Lady Bird Johnson, the First Lady, was the bill's symbolic sponsor. As we don't want to create ugly advertising, and can't conceive of disrespecting a woman named Lady Bird, we have been extremely careful to make Absolut's outdoor advertising as tasteful as its indoor advertising.

This passion for an often overlooked and underloved medium led to our "build-to-suit" strategy. We thought: Let's create spectacular sites in significant markets where the location is critical and integral to understanding the creative idea. Philosophically, this wasn't too different from the city series in magazines. And if by chance one of our generic ideas was great, then we could use it in any city.

ABSOLUT FEUERMAN Actually, Absolut's first outdoor advertising had wheels on it. On top of a flatbed truck, underneath a transparent Lucite cube, the resin sculptures of Carol Feuerman rolled around the streets of New York City. These were life-sized, and lifelike, models drinking Absolut cocktails. Feuerman is an artist well known for her hyperrealist sculptures. And Absolut became the vodka that literally pulled up to your front door.

ABSOLUT NEW YORK New York City is famous as an "apartment city"—and small apartments at that. But could we actually mount a real-life, real-size apartment on a Times Square billboard? Of course we could. Aren't there any tough questions out there?

Jackie End, a classy, charming, and witty lady, still fresh as a daisy after a few decades in the ad business, teamed up with Bill Montgomery, a Miami Ad School graduate, fresh

as a pumpkin, to "build" this ad. The idea was simple: furnish a billboard with actual furniture, as if it were a New York studio apartment: tiny kitchen, bathroom, and TV set included.

We invited IKEA, the retailer (coincidentally, from Sweden) to participate. Their chief designer, Thomas Carlson, was so excited he insisted on designing the entire apartment and providing all of the furniture at no charge.

(Not so) obviously, you can't just glue furniture to a billboard six stories up and hope it stays up. It had to be hollowed out, weatherproofed, and anchored so that we wouldn't wind up on the cover of the *New York Post* for pelting pedestrians with armchairs. Plus, it had to be wired so the TV and lights would actually work. (I don't recall if the toilet actually ran.)

Of course, this was in New York City, not the easiest place to get things done. We needed building permits, crane permits, pedestrian permits, etc. To accomplish all this, we hired what must be the only company in America who does this stuff (yikes, there's a plug): Atomic Props in Minneapolis. They've done these constructions, or what they describe as "fabrications," since 1985, and really know their nuts and bolts. The sales and marketing director there,

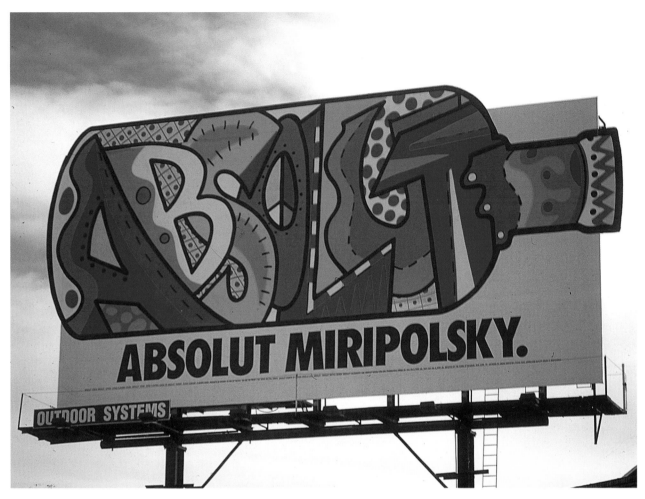

Patty Matthews, takes her business very seriously. I assigned my assistant, Megan Phillips, as our project manager. Her job was to keep it moving, alert me to any impending disasters, and to seek my sage advice when flummoxed.

Megan was a recent Dartmouth grad intent on giving advertising a try. She was very smart, of course, but more important, she was curious, dependable, fun, and funny. Her real passion, however, was horses. Megan aspires to ride in the 2008 Olympics—that's a serious ambition—and has already ridden to victory in a number of international events including the U.S. Equestrian Team Student Riding Nations Cup in Brussels. (Who said ad people weren't multitalented?)

ABSOLUT NEW YORK debuted on Lafayette Street in Soho during the summer of 1999 and quickly became a local landmark. We did have one immediate problem. The billboard company "forgot" to inform us that local residents were upset with this location; some of the more adventurous ones began to pelt the board, almost nightly, with paint bombs. Then each morning someone would have to climb up and scrub. It didn't take us long to hire an overnight, donut-eating security guard who sat in his car "watching" the board until daybreak. That solved the paint bomb prob-

lem. But when our lease ran out at the end of the year, we dismantled ABSOLUT NEW YORK, and cleaned it up for its next performance: Times Square.

Carl Horton had never liked the Soho placement to begin with. "Why put up a great board if no one is going to see it?" he asked, overstating his case just a bit. But, sigh, he was right: this board belonged in the heart of New York—that's where the real crowds would discover it.

ABSOLUT MIRIPOLSKY Andre Miripolsky is one of the more charming characters I've met in my Absolut life. He forgave me for confusing him with another West Coast Absolut artist, Bill Barminski; reminded me his association with the brand dated back to 1990 when he created a piece for Absolut's "Artists of the '90s"; and proselytized that everything in life is about lighting and timing, not a bad pair. Miripolsky created a billboard in San Francisco that was displayed at Eighth Street and Braxton for two full years. I don't remember if it hung that long because we were hypnotized by the art or if we simply forgot it was still there.

ABSOLUT MIGRATION It's always a mistake to destroy giant birds. At least ten years before ABSOLUT MIGRATION flew into the West Side of Manhattan;

TBWA had created a billboard in Los Angeles, California, for Bombay Gin that employed two dozen larger-than-life bluebirds, cardinals, and robins. The theme of that campaign, also authored by Geoff Hayes, the father of the Absolut campaign, had been: "Nothing Attracts Like Bombay Gin." The board featured birds that arrived weekly and stayed until the entire board was occupied. In the intervening decade the birds lived in a warehouse in Colorado waiting for their next liquor gig. That turned out to be the introduction of **ABSOLUT MANDRIN**. (If you're interested in renting these birds for your next party contact *marilyn.kirk@tbwachiat.com*.)

ABSOLUT ART GUYS The Art Guys are two perform-ance/conceptual artists/characters from Houston, Texas. These guys—Jack Manning and Michael Galbreth—have collaborated for over twenty years. They take neither art nor themselves too seriously, and they create some pretty amus-ing sculptures, installations, and videos.

One of their favorite projects was "1,000 Coats of Paint." They took ordinary objects: a telephone, a hammer, a banana—you get the picture—and over several months applied 1,000 coats of paint. Each successive coat was a different color so that you knew they were actually paint-ing. By the end of the project, there would be more paint than object.

The Art Guys performed their paint magic for Absolut

on boards in Miami and Los Angeles. We had to be careful about these locations; as you know, paint drips. I remember one parking lot owner who was very apprehensive. I think account director Pete Callaro had to give him "nervous insurance" to use his space. But in the end we showed that Absolut hadn't lost its art nerve—it was still willing to attempt the outrageous and outrageously funny.

ABSOLUT L.A. Joseph (Joey) Mazzaferro arrived at TBWA\Chiat\Day in late 1999 as the new Absolut creative director. An art director, he was hired by the Agency's exec-utive creative director, David Page, who had been at TBWA only long enough to drink a grandé cappuccino. (Incidentally, for a full TBWA creative director genealogy chart, see page 271.) Joey had met Page at an ill-fated tour of duty at M&C Saatchi, but had stayed in touch after he went to Messner Vetere Berger McNamee Schmetterer Euro RSCG. (That was the real name of the agency. They needed two receptionists to say it. The first one would run out of breath.) There, he worked on the Volvo and J.P. Morgan business, developing a reputation for beautiful, well-conceived work. Joey arrived with his partner, David Corr, a gravelly voiced writer, and a motorcycle maven. Odd couple.

The inspiration for **ABSOLUT L.A.** was the well-known saw that actors and actresses would do nearly any-thing to get their headshots in front of casting directors. For

instance, they hover at the Mondrian Hotel's Sky Bar on Sunset Strip—passing out photos as indiscriminately as take-out Chinese menus on Manhattan's Upper West Side. Or they post them in Laundromats where agents presumably have time to kill between the wash and the dry.

Billy Albores, the ubiquitous TBWA art buyer, contacted Sheila Manning, an L.A. casting agent, for her help. She provided a stack of 4,000 headshots from which Joey selected about 200 different ones. These "heads" then had to get the permission from their photographers for the image to appear on a billboard—as it's pretty unlikely that those rights would have been granted beforehand. Each shot then had to be glued to a vinyl sheet to preserve and protect the photos from the L.A. smog. They were then attached to boards with real pushpins, the production detail that delights me the most.

On "Opening Day," we organized a press table at the foot of the billboard, and Sheila Manning met with aspiring actors, all clutching their headshots, of course.

ABSOLUT ALTERNATIVE Do you remember the California energy crisis of 2001? The state had recently taken responsibility for purchasing electricity from the power companies. At the time, I recall, prices had rapidly shot up, catching municipalities off guard, in the face of severe power shortages. There were widespread brownouts and a lot of angry Californians. One requirement, obviously,

was the need to conserve energy. (Later, it turned out the state had been simply outmaneuvered by Enron-type parasites—there never had been a real "shortage.")

To address the issue both seriously and lightly, Joey Mazzaferro suggested **ABSOLUT ALTERNATIVE**, a billboard powered entirely by the sun. He got the idea from our "Hockeytown" planner, Larry Geis, who informed him that: "Solar Power Is Big." (You have to wonder how much we paid for that consumer insight.) Even if we wanted to, which, of course, we didn't, we weren't going to fake solar power. We had to secure real panels and real storage batteries, connecting them so that the board was actually powered by the sun.

ABSOLUT OUT Absolut has been a friend of the gay community for nearly twenty-five years, long before it became fashionable. Starting with its initial advertising in gay magazines such as the *Advocate*; creating a twentieth-anniversary ad commemorating the 1969 Stonewall Riots; developing a two-year program in *USA Today* that featured an artist from every state, along with a lithograph sale of each image that benefited the Design Industries Foundation for AIDS (DIFFA). (In the interest of full disclosure, a portion of the proceeds from this book—and my previous one—go to the American Foundation for AIDS Research [AMFAR].)

So no one accuses Absolut of being a Johnny-come-

lately to the Cause. Rather, we hear compliments like this one from Stuart Elliott, the impish but dedicated *New York Times* advertising columnist: "Absolut stands at the top of the heap as the brand you associate with gay causes. But they don't merely support them; they're a part of Absolut's soul."

ABSOLUT OUT is a fine example of a brand doing "well," by doing "good," perhaps not an original expression, but one I first heard from David Wachsman, Absolut's PR guru in the 1980s. It was conceived specifically as a tribute to all the gays and lesbians who have come out of the closet during the past twenty-five years. In my view, it is really a celebration of everyone who has peeled off a layer of camouflage in their lives to reveal a truer version of themselves.

This billboard started off in Atlanta, traveled to San Francisco during Gay Pride Week in June 2003, and concluded in New York City in October that year in coordination with National Coming Out Week. When the rolling, two-ton billboard arrived in each city, it was posted with its nine doors closed shut. About a week later, these

doors opened to reveal all the clothes, shoes, and other paraphernalia owned by the different archetypes of pre-coming-out: jock, Wall Streeter, body-builder, activist, and drag queen.

Throughout, Absolut partnered with the Human Rights Campaign, the nation's largest organization whose purpose is to ensure that gay, lesbian, bisexual, and transgender individuals can be open, honest, and safe wherever they are in America. Nice mission.

The campaign also included live and online auctions of items donated from the closets of straight and gay celebrities such as Madonna, k. d. lang, Ellen DeGeneres, and Melissa Etheridge.

Incidentally, this ad was created by an army of TBWAers, tall and small, gay and straight, many who had already moved on before it debuted: Arun Nemali and Mike Davison to name two. Thin Bill Montgomery was still here. And Patrick O'Neill, creative director and ringleader, became both the leader and the inspiration for this project.

ALBUM COVERS

chapter five

BY THE LATE 1990S, THE ABSOLUT COMMITMENT TO THE ARTS WAS AS WELL known among Absolut consumers as it was in the "art" world. But in one area—music—we had barely scratched the surface. True, there had been a number of concerts sponsored by Absolut, mostly by the producing team of Pat Phillips and Etore Stratta. Michel Roux had discovered this quirky pair (or more likely, they found him) and it led to some exciting performances by Antonio Carlos Jobim, Stephane Grapelli, and Paquito D'Rivera at New York's Carnegie Hall. Yet, as stimulating as the music was, these were one-time events limited to the listeners present. It was a bit of a satellite to everything else Absolut was doing. Meaning: it had no connection to the plow that was pulling everything else along, the advertising campaign.

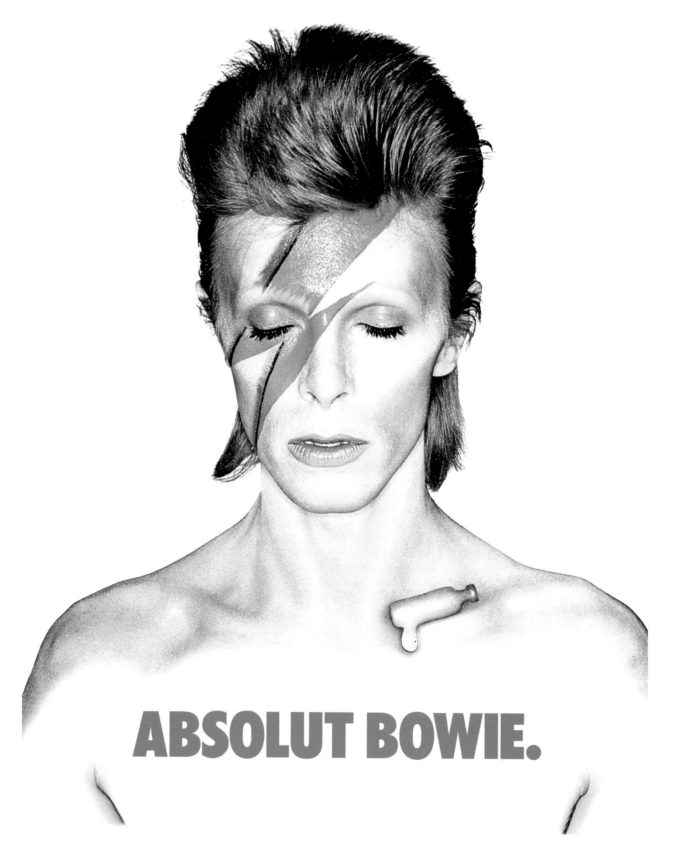

But all that changed, quite by accident, as usual. Tom Godici came to TBWA from Deutsch Advertising, lured by creative director Eric McClellan. Like many creatives, he had freelanced and directed commercials to keep himself sane between the pressure cooker of agency jobs. Tom was originally a designer, graduating from the School of Visual Arts. In fact, one of his early jobs was at CBS Records, where he designed album covers for Nils Lofgren and other artists.

At TBWA Tom was asked to develop a "quality" campaign, an evergreen agency assignment. He figured that one angle would be to turn up the cool meter for consumers in their thirties—by tapping into the music they grew up on in the 1970s. This music was best expressed through the record albums, specifically; the album covers of that time.

A short historic note is probably appropriate here—my apologies to anyone over the age of forty. Before CDs (and, later, mp3s) swallowed the music business, music was stored on round vinyl discs. They came packaged in cardboard jackets that were often decorated with original art, sometimes more original than the music inside.

Godici envisioned transforming these covers into Absolut ads with the simple addition of a well-placed bottle. They would then be headlined ABSOLUT STONES or ABSOLUT DEAD, depending on the name of the band. Central to the idea was having groups with names that worked well with ABSOLUT. Or as he puts it, "look good next to ABSOLUT." He especially liked (Judas) PRIEST and (Velvet) UNDERGROUND as those headlines appeared exciting and provocative.

But back to the assignment. See, Tom had approached the problem in reverse. He wanted to reach these consumers who were experimenting with higher-priced vodkas such as Ketel One and Grey Goose by doing "quality" advertising and not by doing a hymn to wind, water, and wheat, the ingredients of quality vodka making. (I'm cheating here for the sake of alliteration. Of course there is no wind in vodka.)

Tom tells me now that I handled this situation quite adroitly. (He may have even used that word.) Recognizing that album covers were a great idea but clearly not what the client was looking for, I convinced him to hold the idea for a later meeting.

One of the unwritten rules in advertising is "don't present the right work at the wrong meeting." Once a campaign has been presented it runs the risk of seeming old, stale, used, the next time it's brought up. If you do bring it out

MICHAEL PERSSON: WHAT'S THE BIG IDEA?

again, it's often seen as, "We didn't have any new ideas so we brought back some old ones." And even though the Absolut clients are much smarter than to make that judgment, the campaign still didn't belong in the meeting.

Well, we didn't develop, let alone sell, a stirring quality campaign that year. (More on that in a few chapters.) And Tom Godici was no longer at the Agency when we finally presented the album cover series the following year. Sadly, he had moved on to Ogilvy & Mather as a creative director on the IBM account.

(I mention Tom's new work to reinforce both his talent and versatility, typical of agency people. To paraphrase F. Scott Fitzgerald, creatives are different from you and me. And it's not just that they're more creative.)

Amazingly, or maybe not so, the campaign survived his departure. Often, when talent departs an agency, unfinished and unpresented work departs, too. Or the ideas are presented as "new" by a different creative team. Rarely is the work presented as fresh—and from the mind of an ex-employee. If you work in an idea environment it's obviously not a good idea to tell clients that your best idea people have left the building for greener, or at least different, pastures. But it's an unavoidable fact of life in advertising. And due to the strength and durability of our

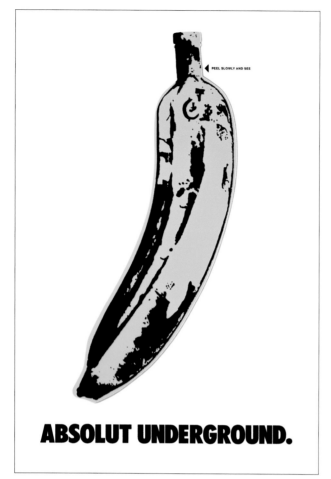

ABSOLUT UNDERGROUND.

ABSOLUT PRIEST.

partnership with Absolut, we could be and were honest about it. It also helped that there was a new client at Absolut with an appetite for big ideas.

Michael Persson arrived at Absolut as its advertising director in late 2000. Being Swedish, he naturally knew about the brand. But since Absolut and other alcohol advertising is forbidden in Sweden, he was largely unfamiliar with the campaign. "I was largely unaware of the variety and depth of the ads, but more important, of everyone's enthusiasm." He heard about the job while at Thorn, the electronics manufacturer, when a friend told him to check out Absolut. Earlier, Persson was at SAS, serving a ten-year stint, where he contributed to the carrier's repositioning as the "Business Airline." (Unfortunately, he should have repositioned the seats in their planes because they're among the most uncomfortable in the sky.) But Michael has a fondness for big ideas, so he arrived at the right terminal.

In many respects, generating the campaign idea and selling it to Absolut proved to be the easy part of getting it done. We had high aspirations as to the musicians whose albums we wanted in the campaign: the Rolling Stones, the Beatles, Led Zeppelin, the Who, the Doors, Jimi Hendrix: all the great bands of our target's adolescence and, naturally, my dizzy youth. It was up to our crack art buyer, Billy

Albores, to find these people and wrangle a deal.

Art buying is an underappreciated department. It requires a rare blend of business and creative skills. Art buyers are responsible for convincing photographers, models, artists, and celebrities to create, perform, or sign away their name or likeness in ads that they may not want to appear in for less money than they're willing to accept. But Billy Albores is much more skilled than I've given him credit for, if only because he actually gets the job done, doesn't complain, and is a nice guy to boot. Plus he (sometimes) laughs at my jokes.

Any ad is difficult to publish if you need someone else's permission. Here, I knew it was particularly challenging because we would need the permission of the recording artist and band members; the album cover artist; and the company that produced and distributed the album. As Billy made it clear from the start, "Rock and roll stars don't sit at desks and keep normal business hours." The things you take for granted.

The corollary to Billy's line is also my favorite business expression: "The next best thing to a "Yes" is a fast "No." Emphasis on fast. As I indicated, we had set our sights very high. And getting feedback from the agents was like squeezing the last toothpaste out of a tube. We had to be

ABSOLUT JOHN & YOKO.

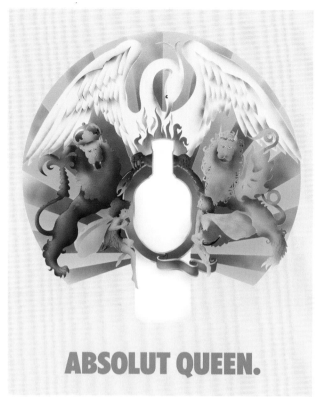

ABSOLUT QUEEN.

patient and live with a dribble at a time.

We were also getting strong rumblings that everyone wanted to be paid a lot of money. Millions. Imagine that. See, being Absolut, there was an assumption that we were rich and would spend accordingly. My thinking had been to create a reasonable budget, and allocate the same outlay for everyone, a method that we've used successfully in the past for writers and artists. Failing that, there are lots of bands out there, so we would just cross off a name and move on to the next. After all, we were offering something of value, too; wide exposure in a respected international advertising campaign and (this was a big "and") the opportunity to sell more of the albums we would feature.

The Rolling Stones were interested . . . but their deal with Budweiser prohibited them from playing with any other alcohol beverages. It took us six months to discover that one piece of information.

As it turned out, Madonna, Kiss, the Clash, and Billy Joel were all beyond our budgets. Several bands, living and dead, declined because of past problems with substance abuse. Led Zeppelin was on vacation in Africa but promised to get back to us. (We're still waiting.)

ABSOLUT BOWIE Just when we were starting to have doubts about the viability of the campaign, David Bowie said yes. It was a perfect match. Bowie, like Absolut, has spent his career inventing and reinventing himself, donning different personae, anticipating and leading both fashion and musical trends. While a more obvious album choice

might have been Ziggy Stardust, the tongue-in-chic-sci-fi-glam album (OK, I promise: no more hyphens for the remainder of this paragraph) that launched Bowie into international rock stardom, Aladdin Sane, was irresistible. It was, we reasoned, both significant music AND a great album cover—showing the orange-haired Bowie and the "amoeba globule" resting, but also oozing, on his collarbone.

ABSOLUT BOWIE was launched in New York on September 5, 2001.

ABSOLUT JOHN & YOKO We were scratching our heads as to how to catch the bigger fish. Since these ads were born to run in Rolling Stone magazine we arranged a meeting with Jan Wenner, the founder and editor in chief, who knows everyone in the music business and was eager to help. Wenner's office is reached after walking a cover corridor: a very impressive display of every Rolling Stone cover since its humble beginning as a tabloid newspaper in 1967. I remember reading Hunter Thompson's outrageous tales of "gonzo" journalism when I was in high school, particularly *Fear and Loathing in Las Vegas*.

Wenner was very cordial and willing to help. He opened the door to someone so special we hadn't even thought we could get: Yoko Ono.

A meeting was arranged through her lawyer, Peter Shukat, and took place at Yoko's office at the Dakota on New York's Central Park West. Joey Mazzaferro and I nervously arrived at the appointed time, and removed our shoes as instructed. Her office was filled with art and photography: Warhol, Haring, and Basquiat. We had brought with us layouts Joey had prepared for the three albums she had collaborated with John: Plastic Ono Band, Mind Games, and Two Virgins. Each one of course had the requisite Absolut bottle.

Yoko told us that the Plastic Ono Band and Mind Games covers were meant to be just record covers, whereas the Two Virgins cover was not just a cover but a statement of its own. Graphically, it stood out as well. So we all gravitated toward Two Virgins. Yoko also made it a condition that we use the back cover, which was John and Yoko displaying their backside, naked.

None of us, even in the stretchable world of ad-land, would have described John Lennon and Yoko Ono's album Unfinished Music: Two Virgins, as a classic rock album. Rather, this joint album of John and Yoko is best described as conceptual, being a recording composed entirely of ambient sounds at their farmhouse. Today, it could be very much at home as New Age. Back in 1968, the critics weren't as open-minded. Of course, the album received a

NEVER MIND THE BOLLOCKS

HERE'S THE

SeX PisTOLS

ABSOLUT PISTOLS.

INXS
★ ★ ★ ★
KICK

ABSOLUT INXS.

sensational reception because of its cover, which Yoko now explains as having been a statement to the world from John and Yoko.

And how did we rationalize the abrupt interruption in our classic rock series? Neal Davies, the recent British import, music expert, sad New York Mets fan and Absolut account director quipped, "We'll declare this the 'Beatles Exception.'"

ABSOLUT UNDERGROUND We returned to our rock roots with ABSOLUT UNDERGROUND. As in Velvet Underground and Nico. It was one of Tom Godici's original choices. This Andy Warhol–produced record became a seminal rock album for its exploration of some of the darker, more ominous aspects of rock, in particular, drug addiction. Musically, Lou Reed, John Cale, Sterling Morrison, and Moe Tucker's experimentation with sound presaged the arrival of alternative rock. However, it took years to become anything like a best seller. According to critic Martin Johnson, music impresario Brian Eno commented, "Only a few dozen people bought this record, but all of them were then inspired to start their own band." And let's not forget the banana! Warhol created a "real" peel-off skin for the cover that's so striking and memorable that it's still referred to as the Banana Album.

ABSOLUT PRIEST The Judas Priest album, British Steel, confirmed their credentials as Britain's premier heavy-metal band (maybe its only one, too). The album was also their first hit in the USA. Just looking at the hand gripping the blade makes me reach for my Curads.

ABSOLUT QUEEN This album, A Night at the Opera, and its successor, A Day at the Races, were Queen's post–Led Zeppelin–hard rock offerings (with an obvious nod to the Marx Brothers). The 1975 Opera launched Freddy Mercury's band into superstardom. "Bohemian Rhapsody" became the band's signature song. Richard Gray's cover art gave more than a hint of Queen's fantasy-spun, dreamy, and mock-mythological take on rock and roll.

ABSOLUT MILES Miles Davis took a little bit of heat from the jazz purists for Bitches Brew because he had the temerity to create a jazz/rock fusion album. (Aside: why can't hero-worshippers let their heroes evolve to create different stuff? That's their job: invent and move on. Otherwise, they probably wouldn't have become heroes in the first place.) Now considered a masterpiece, this 1969 record featured many musicians—Chick Corea, John McLaughlin, Wayne Shorter—who became stars in their own right. Mati Klarwein's cover was an ode to Black power, Black beauty, and Black magic.

ABSOLUT PISTOLS First, let me put my cards on the table: I never liked punk rock and I still don't. It starts with the word "punk" and ends with all those misplaced safety pins and ghoulish hair colors. But don't listen to me. People who know better, with straight faces and no paper clips attached to their lips, tell me this was one of the most significant rock albums of all time. I do like their snotty, antiestablishment attitude; and they even took on the Crown, the Queen (the real one, Elizabeth II), during the 1977 Silver Jubilee. They originally pictured her on the cover of Never Mind the Bollocks—before the authorities convinced Virgin Records otherwise.

ABSOLUT INXS Australian rock band, INXS, became an international sensation with Kick, this 1987 album. It boasts upbeat, Rolling Stones–type electricity without the dark overtones. And friends tell me the music is great to dance to, although having seen me on the dance floor they say it's not for everyone. Sigh. Nick Egan's cover art is reminiscent of 1960s Mod bands.

ABSOLUT HAGEN Some people confuse Nina Hagen with an ice cream of a similar name. Don't. She's much colder. This album, Om Navah Shimray (meaning: "Can't believe you spent your dough on this, Bud," according to Mr. Davies) was born in East Berlin (that is, East Germany) and is sometimes referred to as "The Mother of Punk." In spite of that, Hagen defies categorization as she lives a life of performing, political activism, and general craziness. But her fame—or infamy—in Germany is undeniable.

COLLECTORS

chapter six

WHEN I WAS GROWING UP IN THE 1960s, I COLLECTED POSTAGE STAMPS. This gangly, bespectacled kid spent hours at the kitchen table soaking cancelled stamps from envelopes, drying them on white paper towels, searching through my "Aristocrat" stamp album—the size of two phone books—for the slightly faded, stamp-size (naturally), black-and-white matching photo of it; then attempting to attach it with a gummy stamp hinge. I licked it on one side, then extracted it from my tongue, gently folded it onto the stamp, and placed it in the album, only to have it slide off seconds later. Then tried again. Who said stamp collecting wasn't hard work?

TODD VILLMER, "KING OF THE CRAZIES."

I went on to collect baseball cards, coins, matchbooks, photos of people I've hit with pies (I have two), and, today, my collection of Goofy figurines. My point is that while collecting may seem idiosyncratic, it is driven by what other people collect at the time. I don't know anyone who collects stamps these days (although the remnants of my collection can be found in my wine closet), but lots of people still collect Absolut ads.

By the early 1990s, there were already about 250 ads out there. Most could be found by combing through newsstands and library shelves. A minority had appeared only once, increasing their scarcity and value. I met quite a few adults who were scrounging and begging for these ads for their own children, nieces, or grandchildren. They appreciated the ad campaign's wit, worldliness, and sometimes its ability to expand their horizons. "Mom, who is Keith Haring?" more than one parent echoed to me.

I can honestly say that none of the hundreds of parents I've spoken to or heard from over the years accused Absolut of targeting the underaged with our advertising. Of course, we didn't. They simply recognized their children's interest as a byproduct of advertising directed at adults. As we didn't advertise on television, teenagers wouldn't bump into us while they were watching *Friends* or Major League Baseball. And most kids don't read *Vanity Fair*. One mother once told me her child didn't even know the ads were for vodka because they "transcended" alcohol advertising.

The collecting craze isn't just an adolescent phenomenon, either. While I don't want to give the impression that this is AARP territory, I've had the privilege of meeting a few of the collecting grandmas out there.

It's also not just about the advertising. Nearly everything with the Absolut logo is sought after and saved. And except for the plethora of "homemade" T-shirts, usually

FRANK LOPEZ, "MR. POSTCARDS."

found on college campuses, the vast majority of this Absolut treasure chest was originally manufactured by Absolut itself, or its distributors around the world. How the collectors acquire all this stuff is a bit of a mystery, even to me, given that it was produced for the people who sell and serve Absolut.

Just imagine: Bar glasses, menu cards, stirrers, shakers, pourers, lox slicers. Jewelry including watches, necklaces, pins, cufflinks. Clothing, easily the largest category, naturally including caps, shirts (polo, button-down, T, clingy), ties, and jackets, but also purses, bathing suits (and towels), vests, and formal wear. There are golf clubs, bags, balls, tees. For the home office there are calendars, paperweights, pens, letter openers. Not to mention posters, post cards, and powdered stain remover—I'm not kidding!

VILLMER It actually started out quite innocently. A few Absolut fans found each other through word of mouth.

Like Todd Villmer. Todd is a thirty-five-year-old financial planner and St. Louis native. His parents taught him the collecting ropes early on. Sheila, his mom, is a founder of the 1904 St. Louis World's Fair Society, whose purpose is to keep that Fair alive. Growing up, his home was filled with doodads and doohickeys. Sheila worked at S.D. Warren, a company that produces paper for many high-quality magazines, and she was able to bring home samples to scour for Absolut ads. So Todd got the bug late in high school. And when he read somewhere that Madonna collected the ads, well, his fate was sealed.

In 1995 he started The Absolut Collectors Society. Its purpose was to track ad sightings and merchandise around the USA. They published a monthly newsletter that in its prime reached 2,500 subscribers. They also met periodically to exchange Absolut gossip and trade ads to fill the holes in their collections.

DAVID AND CHRISTINE BELL, ENTREPRENEURS.

Todd appears to be perfectly normal when you meet him. He has a career, he almost got married once, and he owns a home. But it's filled with $50,000 "worth" of Absolut stuff, a veritable Absolut museum. He's also often described as the "King of the Crazies" among the collectors. He doesn't disagree. "That could be me. It's good to be King," he says, quite purposely mimicking Mel Brooks.

While I've known about the underground and above-ground flea markets for Absolut paraphernalia for years, I didn't realize that there was a virtual hypermarket for these goods passing over the Internet. But what the Internet created it also tore asunder. While it made it possible for fans to find and trade with one another, it was just a hop, skip, and a jump to the next evolution: eBay. Once eBay took off, everything had a price tag, and every ABSOLUT L.A. ad had a "value," or at least a price, based solely on what one collector was willing to pay.

LOPEZ Frank Lopez is a forty-eight-year-old compliance manager at Chevron/Texaco in San Francisco. His friends call him "Mr. Postcards" as a salute to his set of 1,300 Absolut postcards. (For comparison: I might have 20 in my desk drawer.) Frank also collects turtle knickknacks,

reptile and amphibian tchotchkes, and (smile!) stamps. He happily recalls the "early" days of 1998 when the Ad Society would actually get together as a group. "It was great fun just meeting the other collectors and swapping ads. I was reminded there were other folks like me and together, this was a real community. But eBay changed all that. Quickly, it got expensive."

BELL Capitalism abhors a vacuum. The "paying" collectors found the sellers who were eager to part with any Absolut item if the price was right. David Bell, from Landing, New Jersey, became both. His collection started innocently enough in 1997: "I thought the ads were cool." He combed the magazine aisles at Barnes & Noble, paying for the magazines containing the Absolut ads he needed. "I have no patience for the Absolut thieves who rip the pages out of the mags." Over the past few years he estimates having spent $40,000 on Absolut stuff of all stripes. He created a Web site (allabsolut.com) not so much for e-commerce but as a way to keep track of his own collection, to accidentally prevent buying duplicates. Bell says his wife, Christine, is very supportive, helping to acquire and keep stock. She must be: they were even married in the Absolut Americana

MURIEL LIPSCHITZ, "ABSOLUT ACE."

MICHELLE CHUMASH, ABSOLUT TEETOTALER.

Gallery in St. Augustine, Florida, owned and created by Michel Roux. It's common for family members to pitch in on the Absolut treasure hunts; apparently, the family that collects Absolut together, stays together.

CHUMASH I don't want to give the impression that collecting is exclusively a male preserve. Consider Michelle Chumash of Matawan, New Jersey. Michelle began collecting as a Penn State student in 1990. While not a drinker—either then or now—Michelle hung a variety of alcohol ads in her dorm room before focusing solely on Absolut. It was "cheap wallpaper." I'm tempted to say she enjoyed Absolut without the risk of a hangover, but that's unfair both to Michelle and Absolut. Like many Absolut fans she joined the Absolut community, or movement, without any side effects.

LIPSCHITZ Then there's Muriel Lipschitz, the self-described "Absolut Ace." Muriel, 50ish, is a married mom in New York's Westchester County. A full-time literacy teacher in the New York City schools, Muriel has spent the last decade assembling a 2,300-ad collection. "They're all different, too. Not seven copies of 'ABSOLUT This.'" Muriel got hooked when she scavenged for ads for her niece, Stephanie. But when Stephanie stopped collecting, Muriel started in earnest. She's slightly embarrassed as to how much money she's spent over the years on her collection. Her husband, Lawrence, has been a huge help, schlepping Muriel to all the research haunts, and he doesn't need to know how much the hobby has rung up. Yet, Muriel is also a real ad detective. She'll search the microfilm archives in her local library for her prey. For instance, she knew that ABSOLUT 4TH/ABSOLUT 5TH had appeared in the *New York Times* near July 4th during the 1980s. Therefore, very

COLLECTORS CONVENTION. Just some of the lunchers at the Pop Art Gallery in NYC, circa 1998 (l-r): Mike Balz, Harriet Clay, Dave Zaglauer, Sherry Reeves, Todd Villmer, Pat "Grams" Zisook. In front: the always low-key Michelle Chumash.

reasonably, she combed the files for ALL the issues of the Times published near the holiday for several years until she found it. With the exact date in hand, Muriel contacted a company called Historical Archives and purchased a copy of the issue for $45. That's perseverance.

Muriel says she's made all sorts of friendships through this hobby. Online, she's met collectors in Canada, Arizona, and the Czech Republic. Her Arizona friend seems to have a special connection to ads that appear in Korea. (It must be the proximity to Seoul.)

What does Absolut think about the collecting, trading, and selling phenomenon? They neither encourage nor discourage it. They require visitors to their Web sites to confirm they're of legal drinking age, as nearly all spirits companies do. They do not provide ad reprints to consumers who request them. But they do protect and police their various trademarks, which often means pursuing companies and individuals who violate them.

From stamps to baseball cards to Absolut Christmas ornaments, interest in specific collectibles waxes and wanes. Unless the younger sibs, children, or grandchildren of these collectors take up the hobby, the ad binders will head to the proverbial attic. Yet, when the value of these collections rise, as they inevitably will years from now, the Todd Villmers and David Bells will be smiling. I hope the collectors will find their collections intact, where they parked them. I still don't understand why my mother jettisoned my baseball card collection, especially that rare Pete Rose rookie card. It must be somewhere on Long Island.

'Sam' Lewis
10/13/00

1. cushion
2. cutlery
3. butcher
4. good-bye
5. bushel
6. soot
7. absolutly   absolutely
8. fiery
9. crackled
10. comparisons
☆ courage ✓

SAM'S SPELLING TEST

YOU CAN'T MAKE THIS STUFF UP.

Back in 2000 when my son, Sam, was not quite nine years old he took a spelling test at school. On the ten-word test he spelled all but one word correctly: absolutely. He forgot the e. I honestly hope this isn't representative of American schoolchildren.

CINEMA

chapter seven

BACK IN 1997, ABSOLUT MAGAZINE ADVERTISING WAS STILL KING: IT ACCOUNTED for 90 percent of the total budget, with the balance going to outdoor advertising and a kiss to the Internet. This was because print—magazines and, to a lesser extent, newspapers—were still the most effective ways to reach the ever expanding Absolut audience. We could slice and dice the audience geographically, demographically, psychographically, and of course, editorially. And while we didn't advertise in the largest circulation magazines such as *Reader's Digest* (which doesn't accept liquor ads) or *TV Guide* (not exactly an Absolut fit), we did advertise heavily in *Time*, *Newsweek*, *Sports Illustrated*, and *People* to name a few.

But we still sought out new and untried little magazines, those with circulations below 100,000 and sometimes well below, such as *Radar*, *Nest*, *Flaunt*, and *Beep*. As Absolut continued to grow under the Seagram umbrella, we understood the importance of these niche publications and the people who read them.

But not everyone reads magazines, and we knew we had to keep exploring new ways of reaching potential Absolut customers. It was time to open another new media door.

The individual at The Absolut Company in Stockholm who initiated this effort was Peter Bunge-Meyer. All his friends call him Peter Bunge (pronounced: Buhn-Ga). Peter's a quiet, thoughtful, and brainy character, who was often underestimated because of his reserved manner. He wouldn't shout back at the loud Americans—either it wasn't his disposition or it just required too much energy.

Peter had worldwide marketing responsibilities, but he had Mexico on his mind. While every market paled in comparison to the Absolut engine in the USA, Mexico was growing quickly because of a combination of good distribution, a strong TBWA office (our first in Latin America), and consumers itching for premium, status-driven products like Absolut. However, it's not a good place to reach the cosmopolitan population through magazine ads. The offerings are thin and the consumers aren't big readers. This insight, from our crack strategic planner, Jean Vaughn, at Teran/TBWA sent us to the movies.

To paraphrase Willie Sutton, the 1950s Boston bank robber, "That's where the consumers are." (When a judge asked why he robbed banks, Willie's response was, "Because that's where the money is!") The sophisticated Mexico City population socializes at cinema megaplexes and shops, eats, and drinks at the cafés and clubs that surround them. Thus, the cinema assignment was born: create commercials to appear in movie theaters.

Cinema commercials are really just big TV commercials. They appear on screens that are hundreds of times as big as your average twenty-five-inch television. They're shot in 16mm or 35mm film (instead of video) to provide the sharpest and most vivid pictures, and boast great sound systems. They're typically longer, too: two, three minutes isn't unusual. But in the end, they're still stories, moving pictures and sound. Laughs, sighs, cries; blood, mud, guts, and cocktails. Like I said, big TV commercials. And big budgets to support them.

Ad agencies can be dangerous places when a television assignment for any client appears. Despite all the chatter about New Media (the Internet) and the endless array of communications vehicles (a popular phrase in the business, probably because it implies motion), the creative people I know don't get excited about designing shelf talkers for Wal-Mart. It's still a thirty-second (TV ad) business. With a successful brand like Absolut that's already famous for its print advertising, it can be like an extra jolt of caffeine for an agency. The opportunity to do the very first Absolut spot would make young men and women swoon.

To be honest, (I hate that expression—they should take away my bananas for a week for having used it) this wasn't going to be a real first. That distinction probably goes to an Athens office of a competing agency network that produced some very inexpensive TV spots fifteen years ago. They were literal translations of the existing print ads. For instance, in one twelve-second spot (hey, it's Greece) you'd see roses tossed on an Absolut bottle, accompanied by the sounds of cheering. Then the headline would pop up on the screen: ABSOLUT BRAVO.

Excitable Eric McClellan was the creative director for our first ads. He saw this as a huge opportunity—both personally and for the Agency. As is customary, the assignment was given to several creative teams at once. Presumably, the best idea would win.

But first there was the creative brief to contend with. Lee Polychron had just recently signed up at the Agency as the new account planner. She had a big, broad smile, warm manner, and was eager to make a contribution. Lee was also a little scattered—but that just added to her feminine charm. And she was fearless in a crazed sort of way. Lee decided that a cinema campaign was the perfect opportunity to reveal another side of Absolut; she called it the "Mystic North." It was a chance to turn Absolut inside out and play up the cold, white, mysterious, lonely, wintry feel of Sweden. Brrrr. McClellan thought it was terrific but was also open to other avenues.

"This was the best Absolut assignment: translating the wit and soul of the brand, the campaign, not just Absolut ads on the screen." So said Chris Van O (no one ever used or even knew his full last name) and echoed by his partner Mark Girand. These guys cracked it on the first day but didn't show it immediately—as first ideas are so disposable. Their premise was a simple one. Since moviegoers are a "captive" audience in the theater, munching popcorn, as they wait for the movie to begin, why not trick them by showing a movie trailer for a make-believe movie? Each trailer could be a genre bender—western, sci-fi, romance,

MCMXCVIII   THIS FILM HAS NOT YET BEEN RATED   (((ABSOLUT SOUND)))   ABSOLUT PICTURES comedy—where the goal or secret would be an Absolut bottle. And there would be images of Absolut bottles throughout, maybe in every scene that would be reminiscent of the "other" Absolut campaign, where the bottle is always, well, somewhere. "We could take on every film type," Girand declared. "It's a campaign that could last forever." Where have we heard this before?

But Eric hated it. "It's an idea, but it's not a big, BIG idea. We want a big, BIG idea. Keep working." And so they did. Mark Girand: "We thought 'Mystic North' was a dumb, nebulous direction. But it wasn't going away. Eric wasn't exactly rational about it."

Girand and Van O did a few treatments for the next internal meeting, preceded in part by this tongue-not-at-all-in-cheek description: "The campaign directly leverages the Swedish heritage of Absolut. The themes focus on Swedish mythology and folklore and unexplained natural phenomena of the North…all employing Scandinavian imagery of frozen wastelands of ice, snow-covered glacial mountains, long dark nights, and crystal-clear star-filled skies. By focusing on Absolut's Scandinavian roots and the ancient mysticism associated with this part of the world, we can convey the quintessential attributes of the Absolut brand: cold, pure, northern, crystalline, and noble."

Unfortunately, no one believed any of this drivel was true, except Eric, and of course, Lee Polychron, the strategic author. It was just one big Swedish role-playing exercise. The spots themselves contained prancing Nordic gods and beasts, magical chariots, Valkyries (female warrior servants to Odin, of course), and cave dwellers swigging icy cold bottles of Absolut. Kim Wijkstrom, our Swede in residence, observed, "This work is as relevant to the New York Mets as to Absolut."

So the fake movie trailers idea started looking bigger and bigger. Three spots were prepared for the meeting: "The Welcoming," a Ridley Scott Alien look-alike, featuring an eerie, green-glowing Absolut bottle that you could misinterpret as a spearmint-flavored product; "A World of Secrets," an eighteenth-century period romance starring two doomed English lovers, each trying to connect their half of an Absolut pendant to the other; and "El Botelleros," an action/adventure film in the style of Robert Rodriguez's El Mariachi and Desperado.

Both ideas were presented to the clients. "Mystic North" never had a chance. While the Swedes are very respectful and celebrate the legends and rituals of their past, they're not as interested in the Hollywood version we had in mind.

Not to mention that they never warmed up to the Swedish coldness. Peter Bunge hammered the last nail in this coffin: "I was always afraid of the Vikings when I was growing up." But they did embrace the trailers—promising an Absolut bottle in nearly every frame was not a bad selling tactic—so it was off to the producers.

Actually, it was off to the directors. We approached the real Ridley Scott. He was only interested in doing the three trailers as a package. And he wanted $8.2 (!) million to direct all three. Like many clients, Absolut didn't want to put a price tag or budget ceiling on this job; but we certainly knew it wasn't $8.2 million. The budget turned out to be $1 million.

We decided to concentrate on "El Botelleros." It seemed affordable and still potentially very exciting to make. After a half dozen other dead leads, someone suggested Sam Rami. Rami was then largely unknown except to the army of fans of his "Dead" movies: Evil Dead and Evil Dead 2. (He has since directed both Spiderman films and A Simple Plan, among others.) But he had directed TV commercials, so we knew he was comfortable with the shorter medium.

STRANGER Renamed, "Hey Stranger!" the trailer was shot on location in the Los Angeles desert over three days in the summer of '98. It "starred" Argentinean actor Ivo Cutzarida as The Stranger, Alex Morissen as Jennifer, and John Saxon as the villainous Cole. (Saxon, a veteran of dozens of screen westerns, made the unusual request—to us novices—for "enhanced pants." I'll let you figure out what those are.)

The story opens with The Stranger walking into town, seeking relief from the burning desert sun. He's carrying a mysterious black case. Everyone, especially his long-lost love, Jennifer, wants to know, "What's in the case?" (I'll also let you figure that one out.)

Ivo Cutzarida didn't speak a lot of English and fortunately didn't need to. Cole did most of the talking, asking Jennifer, "Are you ready to kiss me now, honey?" He got his answer later in the film, as Jennifer aims a huge pistol at him and spits out "Kiss this!" as he bears down on her in a speeding tractor trailer.

The little film is filled with quick cuts of kisses and danger, startled horses and scary explosions, and lots of obvious and not so obvious Absolut bottles. Peter Bunge told the press that "part of the fun is inviting the viewer to discover all the bottle's appearances." As for the mysterious case, I suggested we prepare one version that didn't end with a bottle in the case. Surprisingly, it turned out to be everyone's favorite. And Eric McClellan came up with the

ABSOLUT PICTURES "company" for the opening and closing of the film. "This was the best thing I've ever done in advertising," Eric confided to me. Given all the Sturm und Drang between Eric and the creatives, I was glad he liked the finished product. The film debuted in Mexico City on sixteen screens in spring 1999.

Mr. Album Covers, Tom Godici, was reunited with Mark Girand to develop the next trailer. For those keeping score, the original alternates, "The Welcoming" (the sci-fi take-off) and "A World of Secrets" (the period romance) were consciously or unconsciously eliminated because they were, yes, you guessed it, stale.

BEAT CRAZY Godici and Girand wanted to make a movie about the club life in Ibiza, Spain. (As we had to practically shoot an entire movie to edit sufficient scenes for the trailer, nobody thought it odd that Absolut was now in the movie business.) Apparently, Ibiza is famous for its stadium-sized discotheques and dusk-to-dawn drinking, dancing, and drugging. (As I've led a very sheltered life in Westchester County, this was news to me.) The idea was to create a gangster movie where rivals compete for control of the riches of the Ibiza nightlife. Thus, "Beat Crazy" was born: The story of two DJs, Tony and Shep, who return to Ibiza, their home during their heyday in the 1980s.

There, they have to restore a shell of a club to its former glory, and battle a local big shot who, surprisingly, is named "Mr. Big." His daughter, Catherine, digs Tony, which keeps Mr. Big's anger small, but not Colin, the local king of promotion, whose own bar, Queens, is the sight of a confrontation between Shep and Colin. This is just the beginning of a series of comic but brutal scenes that unfold before our heroes get the music, the girl, and the money. As Godici now points out, "There's no such thing as a nice gangster." And perhaps his sociology is correct. But in the hands of the director, Tarsem, whose most famous credit up to then was the highly regarded music video for R.E.M.'s "Losing My Religion" and since then, the not so highly regarded Jennifer Lopez film *The Cell*, the violence was clearly over the top. And it didn't help that Tarsem arrived in Ibiza for the shoot having been heavily influenced by the movie *Lock, Stock, and Two Smoking Barrels*.

The client was caught off guard in many respects. I telephoned Absolut's president, Goran Lundqvist, from Ibiza to report on the shoot. His response was, "What shoot?" Apparently, Peter Bunge had kept his management slightly in the dark. As a veteran of keeping managements in the dark when assuming certain responsibilities I could sympathize. But it didn't bode well for the trailer.

The early rough cuts featured nearly everything that would make a client nervous: A kidnapping with Shep locked in a trunk; a gangster smacked in the face by a swinging Men's Room stall door; pointed guns; sex on a mechanical bull. Worst of all, there were too few visible Absolut bottles.

This led to what seemed like—because it was—an interminable series of edits. One, dubbed the "Phoenix 90," was a ninety-second version presented to TBWA management—who by now were also freaking out—in, you guessed it, Phoenix, where they were making a new business pitch. Godici believed that this version contained a "palatable amount of violence." Screening this again, four years later, he's right. But we had dug ourselves a sinkhole that just kept getting deeper.

Well, we finally came up with a squeaky clean version of "Beat Crazy." But not before we failed the British Movie Censor Board (not their real name, but also not far from the truth), overspent the budget by 50 percent (which the Agency ended up paying), and made the client question our taste and judgment, which is like being a teenager who "steals" the family car for a joyride, and is never looked at quite the same way again by his parents. (I speak from first-hand experience.) In fact, it was two years before we were invited to do the next trailer. Yet, with time on my side, it's not a bad little film. I mean, trailer.

Even so, the trailers were original and seemingly successful. Audiences in Mexico and a few additional Latin American markets were enthusiastic. Distributors were happy with the program. And Ann Stokes, Absolut's Little Engine That Could, had struck a bargain with the Devil to keep the program going: if the Agency could produce two new trailers for the price of one (and not one inflated, over-budgeted one, either) then the project would continue.

By now, nearly all the players in the previous disaster had left the Agency. Plus there was a new producer, Nathy Aviram, to keep everyone on the straight and narrow. Nathy (pronounced "Notty") had joined TBWA in early 2000, in time to vacuum up much of the "Beat Crazy" mess left behind by his predecessor, John Garland.

The new creative directors, Dallas Itzen and Patrick O'Neill, had joined TBWA a year earlier, first as a favorite freelance team, and then promoted in a typical agency putsch. Dallas and Patrick had already been a very successful team for ten years, especially at Deutsch, where they had worked on Ikea—our Swedish retailer friend—among others. But this was a different kettle of fish; free-lancers generally don't take their work headaches home

with them. Creative directors have to.

Once again all of the creative teams were drafted for the assignment. Many thought Joseph Mazzaferro had the inside track, if only because of his position as Absolut creative director. But Joey ignored this distraction, as he always did, and just plowed ahead. And so did Andrew Golomb and his partner, Tom Christmann.

Andrew, an art director and designer, had joined TBWA in 1999. Or 2000. He's not sure. You get the impression this is just the kind of stuff he doesn't keep track of. But he does recall, even a little proudly, being creative director David Page's first hire. Less proudly, he remembers that nearly every one of his writing partners was fired during his time at TBWA. Andrew refers to himself as "Typhoid Andrew." (An obvious reference to "Typhoid Mary" Mallon, the cook who spread typhoid fever around New York in the early 1900s without ever suffering it herself. Who said this book isn't filled with interesting stuff?)

To their credit—and to account management's dismay—creatives often reinvent assignments. They don't want to do what's been done before, even when there is wide creative latitude. Not surprisingly, there was already a movement afoot to kill, or at least maim, the trailers. "Tom and I wanted to make a funny, oddball movie, not just another genre rip-off," Andrew remembers. Their oddball idea was a movie about sleepwalking, and not just another pedestrian movie about sleepwalking, but "the most anticipated movie about sleepwalking in years." From the start it was titled, "Good Morning, Mr. Grubner."

GRUBNER The story is simple: By night, Jim Grubner has a crappy job: he drives a forklift truck in a warehouse. But during the day he's a successful business executive, dates the boss's daughter, and plays a mean game of tennis—all with his eyes closed, naturally, because he's sleepwalking.

Nobody honestly thought the clients would approve this idea. It was just too weird. But Michael Persson was intrigued, and Ann Stokes was stoked (sorry). From a Swedish point of view, maybe the idea wasn't all that weird. The director we wanted, Peter Weir, was interested. He had just directed *The Truman Show*, which starred Jim Carrey as a man with a make-believe life. However, negotiations broke down over the tone of the spot. Weir wanted to play up the comic elements while the team wanted to play it straight. Andrew, self-effacing and not entirely experienced in big productions, grew concerned. "Who were we to disagree with Peter Weir?"

But Nathy put everyone back on track by suggesting Tom DiCillo for director. DiCillo was best known for a very low

budget independent film, *Living in Oblivion*. As DiCillo hadn't shot any commercials, he asked Andrew and Tom to prepare a very tight storyboard, actually a "timed" board that would include the precise length of each scene.

They originally considered shooting in Prague, a popular choice for non-SAG (Screen Actors Guild) productions. (Creatives are notorious for planning shoots in the farthest country that planes can fly to.) Prague would actually have been economical, but the English-speaking talent pool in the Czech Republic is somewhat limited. So, while other teams had gone to Spain and California, Golomb and Christmann went to Toronto . . . for a weekend shoot. John Turturro was initially interested in playing Grubner, but he, too, wanted to play the character with eyes wide open. The part ultimately went to Andrew Donnelly, a stand-up comic and friend of Golomb's.

Ann Stokes chaperoned and proved very helpful. Originally, there was a racetrack scene featuring Grubner driving a Formula One car, eyes closed, of course. But because of any perceived association between drinking and driving, it was written out once on location—and replaced by a tennis scene. "Ann was great," Nathy remembers. "She lets things fly. More like an agency person than a client." Nathy was less successful keeping the peace at the Four Seasons Hotel bar. He had a run-in with the singer from the rock band Depeche Mode, asking him and his party to keep down the noise of their mini-celebration. David Gahan told Nathy, "What do you mean, keep it down? You're like my grandfather!" Nathy, in his thirties and built like a brick house, doesn't resemble anyone's grandfather. He wasn't amused.

CASANOVA Meanwhile, Joey Mazzaferro and his new writing partner, Pete Lewtas, an Englishman, weren't resting. Like a hungry diner contemplating which cuisine to eat that night, Joey thought, "I'm in the mood for Spanish."

Originally contemplating a Mexican soap opera, Joey and Pete concocted a Spanish farce along the lines of a Pedro Almodovar film. It would center around one character, Alfredo, married to five different women—Pascale, Toti, Manuela, Angela, and a fairly obvious transvestite, Lucia—each, naturally, unknown to the others. The plot revolves around the wives' discovery of the very busy Alfredo and their plot for revenge. The title: "Farewell, Casanova!"

Almodovar was, of course, their first choice to direct but wasn't available. Nathy suggested a surprise candidate, Spike Lee. Joey had seen *Girl 6*, Spike Lee's comedy about a phone-sex operator, a few years earlier. Spike had been making movies for two decades, was one of the best-known

directors in the country with credits including *Malcolm X*, *Summer of Sam*, and *She's Gotta Have It*. Why would he possibly want to shoot a sixty-second Absolut film?

"Yeah, this looks like fun," Spike concluded after reviewing the treatment. Joey said he must have arrived at the Agency fifteen minutes after the telephone call. They discussed shooting in Havana, Cuba, before "settling" on Barcelona.

July in Barcelona was pretty hot. But more than the heat, Nathy remembers the coolness between Joey and Pete on the set. "I'd never worked on a shoot before where the members of the creative team weren't talking to each other. But this stuff happens and we just had to move on." That's Nathy, always so darn practical. I figured it was just a case of strong-willed artist-types disagreeing about stuff no one notices anyway.

Doing my best Rodney King imitation, I just wanted everyone to be happy and get along. (What a waste of energy that is.) On the plus side, I had brought along my fourteen-year-old daughter, Amanda. She had a terrific time observing a big-deal film being made. We even appear in the film as extra-small extras in the back of a movie theater where Alfredo and Angela are snuggling.

By spring of 2002, when Joey and his new partner, Lynn Branecky, conceived "Mulit," the zaniness of the movies seemed perfectly normal. "Grubner" and "Casanova" had restored our credibility. They even came in under budget!

MULIT "Mulit" started with a funny haircut; one belonging to country singer Billy Ray Cyrus. See, Billy Ray wears a mullet. Simply, it's a shag haircut, very short in the front, long in the back. Joey's film, "Mulit," tried to provide one possible answer. "My vision for this film was surrounded by the mystery of the origin of the mullet haircut and the intrigue that Bollywood musicals have with worldwide audiences." High concept all the way.

Mulit (Raja Vaid) is a Bombay hairdresser who falls in love with the prime minister's daughter, Nita (Richa Pallod). His jealous rival, in love and hair, is Vikram (Vejay Raaz). He'll do anything he can to ruin Mulit. Vikram reveals the love affair to the prime minister (Anupam Shyam). The PM orders Nita to stop seeing Mulit, but she disobeys, returns to Mulit, and asks him to cut all her hair. Before Mulit can finish, the PM's henchmen throw him into prison, leaving Nita with the half-a-haircut that becomes famous worldwide as the Mulit.

Joey initially wanted Baz Luhrman to direct. (Actually he wanted Stanley Kubrick, but Kubrick had died three years earlier.) Luhrman wanted to make the film in Australia, building a Bombay set. But it just seemed too impractical for everyone. Czech director Ivan Zacharius was interested. And he wanted to shoot in Bombay.

"People would carry apartments on their heads as they walked down the street," Joey reminisces about the city. Making a film in Bombay is no day at the beach. Especially when you're filming in their version of Hell's Kitchen. Work stops when oxen have to cross the road, a frequent occurrence. The product of indoor plumbing often runs down the street. The police regularly shut down the production, "arresting" the location manager until he could be bailed out of jail for 500 rupees (about $11). There was a crew of about 200, perhaps six times as many people that would be necessary, say, in the States. And how did the locals respond when something seemed inexplicable? "That's how it's done in India." Of course, the locals assumed this was a "real" movie; but they couldn't understand why we were making a film about a haircut. They were in good company.

When the shooting shifted to Jaipur in the Rajistan region, the difference was night and day. A (real) king and prince observed the shoot in their palace, where they had entertained the likes of President Clinton and Queen Elizabeth. As Nathy observed, "There were rubies in the walls."

The finished film was much more than a sixty-second trailer. Absolut also produced a twelve-minute-long "real film" that was entered in film festivals throughout the world.

I have spared you nearly all of the ideas that didn't make it into production. Many of them would prompt reasonable people to ask, "What were they thinking?" There was a tendency for people at the Agency to conjure up crazy recipes for these films—combining as many film genres as the skillet could hold. Add Absolut. Shake hard. Half bake. Taste carefully.

"Go Suki Go!" for example, was the story of a young, shy Japanese woman—Suki—who is whisked away from a Tokyo train, appears on a game show hosted by her idol, Chad Sui, wins a trip to the moon, where her every movement is broadcast to Earth, but is stranded due to a technical glitch on her spaceship. In his client pitch Joey called this idea *"The Truman Show* meets *Ferris Bueller's Day Off* meets *My Fair Lady* meets *Lost in Space."*

I'm not making this up. Just ask him.

ABSOLUT 6.0

THE AGENCY IS FREQUENTLY ASKED TO CREATE "GOOD-BYE" ADS FOR DEPARTING executives. When Goran Lundqvist, Absolut's much-adored president, retired in 2001, we were up to the challenge. Lundqvist was a diver on the 1960 Swedish Olympic Team that competed in Rome. Incidentally, he won a silver medal.

QUALITY

chapter eight

DISCUSSIONS ABOUT VODKA QUALITY ARE A FUNNY BUSINESS. THIS IS PARTICULARLY true in the USA where an attempt was made to fully democratize vodka through legal means. In 1949, The Bureau of Alcohol, Tobacco, and Firearms (BATF), a division of the U.S. Treasury, tried to clarify matters by declaring that all vodka had to lack any "distinctive character, aroma, or taste." Doesn't that sound a tad boring, not to mention probably unachievable? (And whose idea was it to link the alcohol with tobacco, and the firearms? What about other products that get men into trouble . . . like perfume, stockings, and fast cars?) But back to the vodka.

While I was growing up, the conventional wisdom was that all vodka was alike. If you were drinking vodka, you should drink the least expensive vodka you could find. (Actually, we said "cheapest," if only because it sounded like even less money than "least expensive"). There were literally thousands of brands to choose from—vodka is inexpensive to make, and doesn't require aging as scotch, bourbon, and other spirits do, so every local package store seemed to have its own house brand. It was always the cheapest in the store, as if they were distilling it in the backroom.

Vodka was born in Russia, of course, about 700 years ago. So nearly all of the products were given Russian-sounding names—for a veneer of authenticity, that is, a "made in Russia" shine. Customers could choose from Georgi, Popov, Smirnoff, Czarist, or Bunnov. All of them were made in America, many in Connecticut, by the leading vodka distributor, Heublein (now owned by the British conglomerate Diageo).

Diageo's leading brand, Smirnoff, is a perfectly decent vodka and is the best-selling vodka in the world. They also produce Popov, a popular-priced brand that sells for several dollars less. Some cynics believe the two are actually the same product, but I don't count myself among them. Smirnoff was actually the cool vodka in the 1950s and 1960s, in an America where vodka was still an experimenter's category. They had a famous advertising campaign, too, with the tagline "Smirnoff leaves you breathless," a reference to vodka's near lack of aroma, in contrast to other breathier alcoholic beverages.

The dynamics of the vodka market changed dramatically—and serendipitously—in 1968, when the Pepsi Cola Company tried to sell Pepsi in the Soviet Union. President Richard Nixon sent Pepsi chairman Donald Kendall to Moscow. The Russians were interested, but all trade between the two countries had to be done on a barter basis. The Russians offered to create an export version of their popular vodka, Stolichnaya, to help pay for the Pepsi. This would be the first real Russian vodka imported into the USA.

Since Pepsi wasn't interested in marketing Stolichnaya in the USA, they approached major liquor companies, including Seagram. Somewhat shortsightedly, Edgar Bronfman Sr. declined, reportedly asking, "Who would buy a Russian vodka in America?" So Pepsi set up its own importing company, Monsieur Henri, to handle Stoli.

"They priced it a few dollars above Smirnoff, and with the perception of quality and coolness, they were off to the

races," according to Richard McEvoy, an industry veteran who later contributed to Absolut's success as USA marketing director at Carillon Importers. Stoli drinkers are a loyal breed. Its taste is often described as "honest vodka." What does "honest vodka" mean? Your guess is as good as mine. But Stoli's real appeal was its perceived authenticity, which its marketers reinforced with advertising that emphasized its "Russian-ness." The ads also emphasized its purity—with images showing the bottle frozen in a cake of ice.

While Stoli opened the door for premium vodka in the USA, Absolut marched right through it. Introduced in 1979, Absolut quickly caught on, proving that an imported vodka brand didn't have to be from Russia to be successful. While the advertising campaign is given the lion's share of credit for the brand's phenomenal success—too much credit, in my opinion—what's often overlooked is the role of the product itself. As Doyle Dane Bernbach's Bill Bernbach said, "Nothing will kill a bad product faster than good advertising."

ABSOLUT PERFECTION The very first ads, that we now clumsily call "Bottle ads," were really quality ads. Take another look at ABSOLUT PERFECTION: Yes, we wanted you to smile when you recognized the halo of an angel—but it's the bottle and its contents that are "perfect."

Seriously, is there a level of quality higher than that? And when you read the copy printed on the bottle, aren't you transported to the "rich fields of southern Sweden" . . . and can't you just imagine the picturesque "old distilleries near Ahus" that have been producing vodka "in accordance with more than 400 years of Swedish tradition" . . . (Hey, maybe they struggled for the first 100 years or so, but you have to figure they had another 300 years to get it right) . . . which has been "sold under the name Absolut since 1879." These are not Johnnies-come-lately to the business of vodka making. These are serious Swedes. (Trust me, I've met them. They don't joke about the vodka.)

This logic worked until about 1995. Up to then, Absolut had beaten off all their competitors with a cultural stick. Literally dozens of Absolut wannabes arrived and departed with their well-designed bottles, imported pedigrees, and tongue-in-cheek advertising. They were also priced at or slightly below Absolut, too, in order to compete directly against Absolut or position themselves as "Absolut quality without the Absolut price."

Ketel One was the first brand to sting us. It's from Holland (Holland!) and was introduced with hardly any spending (for marketing) directed at consumers or bartenders. Priced a couple of dollars above Absolut, about nineteen dollars per 750 ml, it was unafraid to explore unknown vodka territory.

Everyone snickered about Holland: What kind of vodka tradition did they have? But if you examine the bottle today, you'll discover the Nolet family has been making their vodka in Schiedam since 1691. Ten uninterrupted generations later, the Nolets are still making vodka. (Wouldn't you think just one of these Nolets wanted to become a doctor, but got sucked back into the distillery?) But this was just the tip of the iceberg.

In 1996, a small New York importing company, Sidney Frank Importers, introduced a French-made vodka called Grey Goose. Overcoming a slow and rocky start, as is often the case with new products that attempt to be a little different, Grey Goose slowly carved its own vodka path.

What distinguished Grey Goose from existing vodkas was first and foremost its price: nearly $25, well above all the competition. They wanted to make a simple statement with that high price—that they were the best. The bottle is tall, frosted, and windowed, providing a view of geese flying above a glaciered sea. Then there's that bold, audacious name, Grey Goose. (Although to this eye, at least, the goose is white.) Finally, and most importantly, Grey Goose made

a fuss that hadn't been made before: it claimed to be the best-tasting vodka in the world.

Slowly, slowly it caught on. The campaign was led by the ageless and cantankerous Sidney Frank, a veteran of at least fifty years in the liquor business. Sidney enjoys playing the industry rogue. His most recent success had been a decade earlier with Jagermeister, a German herbal liqueur that is a very difficult swallow and, in fact, could win many worst-tasting competitions. But Sidney turned it into a phenomenon, particularly on college campuses, by creating the Jagerettes, a bikini-clad troop of women who roamed from bar to bar spraying cold Jagermeister into customers' mouths.

In 1998, Sidney Frank hired the Beverage Testing Institute of Chicago (BTI) to conduct a blind taste test of 40 vodkas. Each was awarded points for smoothness, nose, and, of course, taste on a 100-point scale. Surprise: Grey Goose achieved the highest score with 96. (Absolut had an 80.) There were nearly 20 vodkas in between, some that I honestly had never even heard of and wondered if they actually existed; Van Hoo (Gesundheit!) was one example. Oddly, these test results were never replicated by BTI—or anybody else.

Grey Goose built its brand on the shoulders of this single test result. They created one annoying ad and ran it hundreds of times—and it worked. Many ad professionals describe the taste test ad as cheesy, gauche, or distasteful. I give them credit; they stayed on message. Grey Goose became what it set out to be: the world's best-tasting vodka. And it proved so successful for Sidney Frank that he sold Grey Goose to Bacardi in 2004 for $2 billion.

What about that taste? I have observed consumers from the other side of the one-way focus group glass for over 20 years. I have heard them (you) discuss their (your) relationship with dozens of products. It should come as no surprise that I have heard hundreds (maybe thousands) of people talk about vodka. You are not Robert Parker–type wine tasters. You are real people who actually buy the vodka. And then even drink it. So what taste do you prefer in a vodka? Vodka with no taste. No smell. No burn. No nothing. Maybe the BATF actually got it right (remember odorless, colorless, tasteless). You want vodka that tastes like water! Or, as close as it possibly can.

Grey Goose comes very close. Certainly, closer than many brands, definitely closer than Absolut. But that is by Absolut design, not by accident.

Absolut vodka is made from winter wheat—and lots of it.

THE NEW YORK TIMES, TUESDAY, APRIL 1, 1997   A17

THE MOST POPULAR AD CAMPAIGN OF ALL TIME NEED NOT RUN FOR ALL TIME.

It was good advertising. It had a good, long run. But everyone knows what must come to all good things.

Ironically, the old ads were, in a way, too charming. Too engaging, really too much fun. They were diverting consumers' attention from a far more important story.

Don't get us wrong, it was right for the time. It was fun and we'll miss it. Gee, it's been 17 years and hundreds of ads since ABSOLUT PERFECTION first ran, way back in 1980. But times change and so must the way we relate to our customers. We think people deserve more; more information about their favorite vodka.

We all know what's on the outside of the bottle (the old campaign certainly saw to that), but now we think it's high time we got to the heart of the matter – it's time to talk about what's inside the bottle.

You are now reading the first ad in the new Absolut Vodka campaign. The first in a series of messages from a company that has a lot to say about vodka.

SO LET'S TALK WHEAT

That's right, wheat. More specifically, wheat from the fields in and around the medieval town of Ahus, Sweden, the birthplace of every single drop of Absolut Vodka. This grain is key to the character of the world's favorite vodka.

Pour a touch of Absolut Vodka into a snifter and savor the aroma. You are experiencing a distillation of the finest grain on earth – golden Swedish wheat, rich in flavor from the minerals and nutrients found in the soil of the fields of southern Sweden. And so it has been since 1879 when Lars Olsson Smith produced the first bottle of what the world now knows as Absolut Vodka.

But it's not enough to have the fields and grow the wheat. It's important to know what to do with the grain once it's brought in from the harvest.

Absolut Vodka is produced using centuries-old distilling expertise and tradition in combination with modern distillation technique, and an elaborate modern purification process called rectification. It's what makes Absolut *Absolut.*

The best vodka is clean vodka. When the spirit is charcoal filtered, which many vodkas are, impurities generated by fermentation and distillation are left behind, and those can wind up in your Martini. Charcoal filtering is a highly inefficient method of removing unwanted impurities.

Rectification, the process used by Absolut Vodka, may be expensive and painstaking – it involves a sophisticated and rare continuous distillation process which runs the vodka through several apartment building-sized columns – but it produces a product unusually free of impurities, while still maintaining the essence of the golden grain of southern Sweden.

This is the secret to Absolut.

BE IT EVER SO NORDIC, THERE'S NO PLACE LIKE HOME

If your vodka is distilled under license in 30 industrial locations around the world, chances are the quality is uneven.

The entire world supply of Absolut Vodka is produced at the same distillery in southern Sweden, in the town of Ahus. Every single drop of water

comes from the same underground spring that has contributed to the mystique of Absolut Vodka for centuries, and so it continues to this day.

Moreover, it is vital for the producer of a great spirit to have complete control of the entire distillation process from grain to glass. Absolut Vodka is just such a spirit.

A FAMILY OF FLAVORS

It's not as easy as it seems. We've experimented with hundreds of possibilities. After all, we're not just producing a flavored vodka, we're producing flavored Absolut!

And our customers have been glad for our efforts. Lemony Absolut Citron (actually a blend of four citrus fruit flavors) is today the world's most popular flavored premium vodka. Absolut Kurant, flavored with the delicate essence of natural black currant, is equally tasty. And our third flavor, Absolut Peppar, is perhaps the most rewarding and unexpected variety in our family.

IT'S NICE TALKING TO YOU

We believe a dialogue with our customers is critical to the vitality of our company. And a dialogue is exactly what we wish to begin, with this new, more informative approach to advertising. So say goodbye to our old voice and hello to our new, customer-oriented style of communication.

Let's start the dialogue right now. Pick up the phone and give us a call with any questions, comments or ideas at 1.800.324.2224.

And remember, it doesn't really matter what's in the ads, it's what's in the bottle that counts.

And that's Absolut.

CALL WITH ANY QUESTIONS, COMMENTS OR IDEAS: 1.800.324.2224.

More than two pounds of this hardy wheat grain is used to make every liter bottle. And while vodka can be made from literally any fermentable product—sugar beets, potatoes, rye, rice, corn, bananas—experts, particularly Swedish experts, agree that the best vodka is made from grain, and wheat is the finest grain for making vodka. Seriously.

To nobody's surprise, Absolut uses Swedish wheat that grows, literally, around the corner from Ahus, where Absolut is distilled. But wheat does have some taste, which can be retained or eliminated through distillation. Absolut has chosen to retain the slightly grainy, even bready flavor to give the product some character. And that's been the recipe for hundreds of years. But in recent years it's become fashionable to wash out as much taste as possible because some consumers believe, or have become convinced, that no taste is the best taste. Why is that?

I think people believe that any vodka taste indicates impurity; that it may even cause or contribute to a hangover. Vodka looks like water, so it should taste like water. And water is refreshing, universal, and without aftertaste.

When I heard a focus group participant ask, "Why doesn't Poland Spring make a vodka?" I realized other people—you, for example—might feel the same way.

But what do you do when your vodka doesn't taste like water, but tastes like, uh, vodka? Short of changing the 400-year-old recipe, Absolut was Absolut. To the best of my memory, no one even considered suggesting a reformulation. After all, Absolut had become a seven-million-case brand worldwide, and the third largest spirit brand behind Smirnoff and Bacardi. Any suggestion to reformulate based on the small but growing super-premium segment in the USA could only bring to mind the classic and infamous marketing blunder made by Coca Cola in 1985 when it introduced "New Coke" and killed (old) Coke. They had done it because research—consumers—told Coke they wanted a sweeter, more Pepsi-like product than the one Coca Cola had been producing for about 100 years. The disaster, though, was created by the research methodology. Coke failed to ask, so consumers didn't mention, that while they wanted a Coke alternative, they didn't necessarily want to say good-bye to "old" Coke.

The second challenge Absolut faced from brands like Grey Goose, Ketel One, and Belvedere was one we could presumably do something about. Each brand wanted to grow big by emphasizing they were small. Small company. Distilled in small batches. Handcrafted. Old-world recipes.

As these "better tasting," more expensive, more exclusive brands rose above Absolut, in effect driving Absolut down the vodka hierarchy, it became clear that we needed to do two things.

First, The Absolut Company developed a product with a taste and price profile to take on these other brands. This ultimately became "level": a vodka introduced last year that offers a perfect balance of smoothness and character but with a taste equal or superior to that of Grey Goose, according to Absolut's own consumer testing.

Second, we still had to show consumers that Absolut was also in this league by emphasizing our own quality credentials. The question was how to accomplish this without messing up the brand image established by the now very famous and successful ad campaign.

ABSOLUT APRIL FOOL Naturally, our first thought was to announce the "death" of the advertising campaign as you knew it, which we did on April 1, 1997 (subtle, huh?), in full-page ads in major newspapers. Getting right to the heart of the matter, the headline read: "The Most Popular Ad Campaign of All Time Need Not Run for All Time." The copy promised lots of wheat, water, and distillation secrets, exclusively, as the ingredients of Absolut ads for the foreseeable future. You could say it was a mock punishment for all the consumers who claimed an insatiable interest in such information.

Once you get going with a "story" like this, it's hard to stop. Copywriter Ray Johnson had a great time misleading readers, and was disappointed that he had to let people off the hook at the bottom of the ad. But he included an 800 number that readers could call to vent. Readers who called were told that it was just a big **ABSOLUT APRIL FOOL**'s joke. Aw, shucks. But, obviously, a single Tylenol wasn't going to wipe away this headache.

ABSOLUT TRUTH Our next effort poked fun at the whole notion of taste tests. **ABSOLUT TRUTH** asked, "Why is it that every brand that pays for a taste test wins? Coincidence? Darn good luck? We don't think so." Indeed we don't. I suspect we were showing our frustration over the effectiveness of the Grey Goose BTI test. So we created our own traveling taste tester, searching the globe for the best-tasting vodka. (I suppose there are more tedious ways to earn a living.) Inevitably, in our taste test, Absolut was the winner. But it became increasingly clear that our underwear was showing. We were striking back—but to what effect? A more substantive approach was called for.

ABSOLUT TRUTH?

WHY *is it that every brand that pays for a taste test wins? Coincidence? Darned good luck? We don't think so. So we thought we'd try our theory out for ourselves. Armed with clipboards, and certain in the knowledge that we'd be racking up untold numbers of frequent flyer miles, we began our quest.* —∞—

SWEDEN — First we asked ten Swedes (who were fishing at the time) if they liked ABSOLUT better than any other vodka. Nine said yes. The tenth didn't answer as he had dozed off. —∞—

GREAT BRITAIN — Next we stopped in London, blindfolded seven pub patrons (who took to it like those proverbial ducks) and asked them to comment on the taste of ABSOLUT. Two were very quick to say it wasn't scotch. Three enthusiastically identified it as a superior vodka and went on to say that those witty little onions would be superfluous. While the last two fell to swearing on Henry VIII's assorted wives that henceforth, ABSOLUT would be the only vodka ever to pass their lips. —∞—

ITALY — Greatly encouraged, we flew to Rome, found two cognoscenti at an outdoor trattoria and asked our question. They sipped the ABSOLUT, watched some women walk by, then sipped again. Suddenly there was much smiling and gesturing accompanied by words like; *'Eccellenza! Superiore! Al Dente!'* and *'Bella! Bella! Bella!'* Clearly we had gotten what we'd come for, so we just ate some Gorgonzola and left. —∞—

Advances in blindfold technology have resulted in improved accuracy at the 110% confidence level.

FRANCE — Hopping over to Paris for further elucidation, our flawed French annoyed everyone and so they refused to comment. However, we were pretty danged sure they appreciated the distinctive taste of ABSOLUT and its incomparable savoir-faireness as they pigheadedly refused to give us back the bottle. —∞—

NEW YORK — Across the ocean, at a dimly-lit club on Manhattan's Upper East Side, everyone was wearing black and we were confronted with a roomful of floating faces. Since everyone was drinking ABSOLUT, we felt a little foolish but asked our question anyway. The response? *'Who let you in here?'* —∞—

CANADA — Further North (and perhaps warmer), we were delighted to discover that the Canadians have such a profound respect for the taste of ABSOLUT, many have proposed it be nationalized. —∞—

CALIFORNIA — Hollywood was our next testing site and it proved to be as conclusive as the others. Dodging waiters who would one day be stars, we interrupted two deal-making moguls quaffing $32 spring water, and asked them to comment on the taste of ABSOLUT versus other vodkas. After several sips, they stopped, stared at each other and said in unison; *'What other vodkas? We love this vodka!'* And indeed, with each sip, their excitement seemed to grow. *'I see a windswept glacier that stretches to infinity.'* said one. *'That's funny'* frowned the other, *'I see acres of undulating golden Swedish wheat.'* Suddenly there was a manic repetition of the phrase, *'High Concept'* followed by talk of a love story set in Sweden and an early Spring release date. After which it was impossible to get their attention. —∞—

JAPAN — Crossing yet another ocean we arrived in Tokyo to find that the national penchant for making things as small as possible had already resulted in a fair amount of popularity for our diminutive 50 ml. bottle. However, for us, it was not about size. *'Yes, it's delightfully small,'* we said, *'but isn't it just the best-tasting vodka ever? Huh? Huh?'* Our efforts were amply rewarded. It seems that in Japan, the simple purity of ABSOLUT recalls the joys of Haiku and certain summer cloud formations as viewed from the base of Mt. Fuji. —∞—

CONCLUSION — *So there it is. In every country and on every coast we visited, the answer was the same. Of all the vodkas,* **ABSOLUT** *had the highest rating for taste. Honest.* —∞—

IF THE SOIL

IS REAPED BARE

OF IT'S FRUIT

WILL IT RISE AGAIN

TO BEGIN

ANOTHER LIFE?

WILL THE WATER

SEEP INTO THE EARTH'S

SKIN TO RISE AGAIN

ONE DAY TO BECOME

SOMETHING GREATER?

DO THE FIELDS OF WHEAT

SING IN THEIR

WAVING SILENCE

IN ANTICIPATION

OF THE FUTURE?

ABSOLUTLY

Photographed exclusively by

Helmut Newton for Absolut Vodka.

ABSOLUTLY

First, we took an arrow out of our art quiver. Helmut Newton, following his Absolut fashion shoot with model Kristen McMenamy, had told Absolut president Goran Lundqvist that he wanted to return to Sweden to photograph the winter wheat. And he was serious. When art director Greg "Spooky" Jenson contacted him, Newton practically boarded the next plane to Ahus. This labor of love and grain ran eight pages long and was distinguished not so much by the presence of the wheat but by the absence of the Absolut bottle (or variations thereof) until the final page.

Perhaps in a salute to another famous Swede, Ingmar Bergman, Newton photographed a farmer looking very much like the Grim Reaper. While this produced a lot of spirited conversations between client and agency, ultimately, the reaper was cut from the ad.

We started to look for a complementary—and complimentary—advertising campaign that could live comfortably with the existing campaign and fortify this twenty-first-century notion of vodka quality. Of course, the creatives all pulled their hair out, whining and moaning about the assignment. On some level, I couldn't blame them. Some

argued this wasn't a quality issue whatsoever. Rather, it was about coolness and trendiness; that because Absolut had become so mainstream and ubiquitous, so well-known—like Nike or Coke—it had just become cooler to order Ketel One. Or Grey Goose. And so on. Absolut, according to this line of thinking, had lost its cutting edge and its "specialness." Fortunately, creative directors Dallas (Itzen) and Patrick (O'Neill) took the assignment seriously and made sure that everyone in the department behaved like adults. (At least for this assignment.)

One idea was to claim an Absolut Shortage. It would even show the wheat fields ablaze in a huge fire as "support." I like to think we yanked it before the meeting because our clients would never have resorted to such dishonesty.

AHUS TOURIST BOARD Joey Mazzaferro's invention of an Ahus Tourist Board was a much better idea. The theme was, "Come to Ahus, it's so nice." It would be a parody of all the rinky-dink tourist campaigns in the world; (think "Visit New Jersey") but at the same time extol the wonders of a visit to Ahus—the birthplace of Absolut vodka.

With tongue firmly dug into cheek, and the copy written in a form of Swede-English, we invited visitors to admire the "Soil so clean you can eat it! But don't!" And "Water so pure you can drink it!" The images showed authentic-looking Swedes just being themselves.

Come to Ahus! It's so nice! One of our most major attractions! Winter wheat! The finest wheat on all the globe! And water so pure, you can drink it! Even before we turn it into Absolut Vodka! Ahus! Just south of Kristianstad!

BUT OF COURSE THE ABSOLUT DISTILLERY! HERE WE MAKE VODKA, YES?

VISIT THE LARS OLSSON SMITH MEMORIAL, FATHER OF ABSOLUT. FREE ADMISSION. NO COST TO YOU.

FOR YOUR FREE VISIT ÅHUS BROCHURE, SEND SELF-ADDRESSED STAMPED ENVELOPE TO:

FREE VISIT ÅHUS BROCHURE C/O ÅHUS TOURIST BOARD ÅHUS, SWEDEN

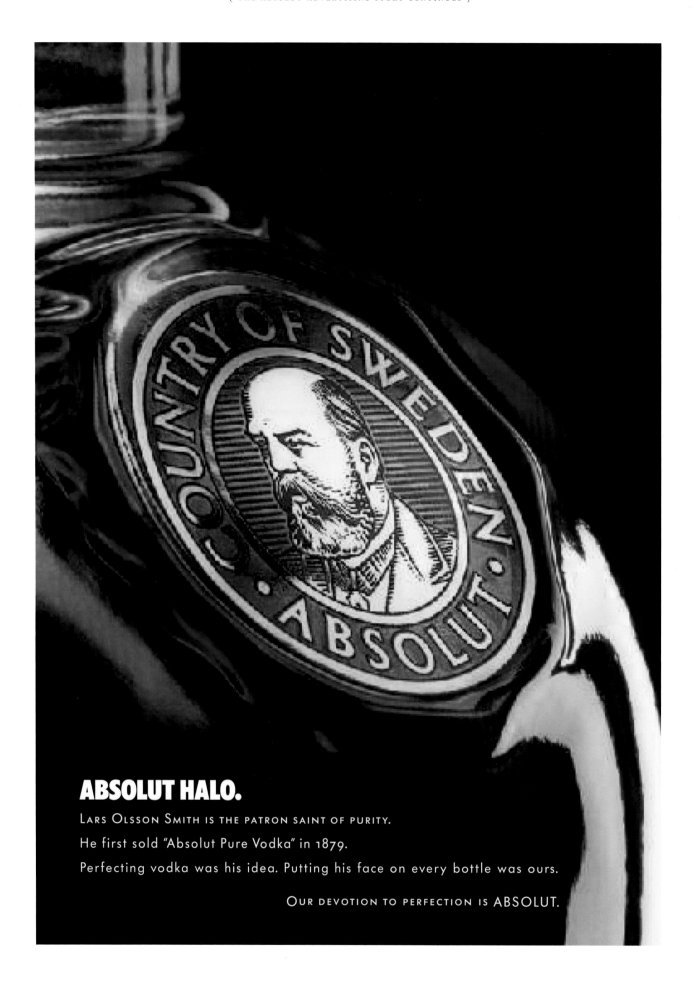

ABSOLUT HALO.

LARS OLSSON SMITH IS THE PATRON SAINT OF PURITY.

He first sold "Absolut Pure Vodka" in 1879.

Perfecting vodka was his idea. Putting his face on every bottle was ours.

OUR DEVOTION TO PERFECTION IS ABSOLUT.

ABSOLUT PATIENCE.

A martini can be made in as little as 63 seconds.

An ABSOLUT martini, however, requires a bit more lead time. 10 months to grow the winter wheat, and 50,000 years for our water source, a bedrock aquifer, to form.

OUR DEVOTION TO PERFECTION IS ABSOLUT.

ABSOLUT ORIGIN.

ABSOLUT DISCERNMENT.

UNLIKE OTHER VODKAS, ABSOLUT IS NEVER CHARCOAL-FILTERED. We fail to see the appeal of a drink poured through scorched wood chips. ABSOLUT distills without filtering, for perfect clarity and a smooth taste.

The charcoal we keep handy for cookouts.

OUR DEVOTION TO PERFECTION IS ABSOLUT.

ABSOLUT INFINITY.

A VODKA MIGHT BOAST THAT IT IS FOUR-TIMES DISTILLED. Five times. Eight. How

ABS

e goal is perfection, big numbers do not always add up.

ed continuously, achieving the perfect balance of character and taste.

OUR DEVOTION TO PERFECTION IS ABSOLUT.

ABSOLUT SANCTITY.

A DILEMMA FOR THE GLASSBLOWER: How does one rinse the bottle that is to hold such a pristine spirit? THE SOLUTION: Rinse with ABSOLUT. Then fill with ABSOLUT.

OUR DEVOTION TO PERFECTION IS ABSOLUT.

It's a wonderful campaign. But, alas, the real Swedes demonstrated there was a limit to how much fun we could have at their expense. Here, we had exceeded it. "You know, we do have feelings," Michael Persson offered, stifling a laugh. What a shame. The campaign feels so Absolut.

One thing about Joey: After you knock him down, he gets right back up again. He just might be the patron saint of absolute patience. By now, it was 2002 and we were still knocking our heads against the wall looking for the "right" quality campaign. People scattered as soon as you brought it up. Hey, where did everybody go?

ABSOLUT HERITAGE When the "Heritage" campaign was born that spring, Joey confessed, "I just wanted to do beautiful shots of the bottle: tight, close and personal." His latest partner (I know: Joey consumes partners like I eat bananas), Andy Hall, married those beautiful shots with what came to be referred to as "nuggets": singularly interesting facts about Absolut vodka.

I think we started with one undeniably interesting fact: Before an Absolut bottle is filled with Absolut, it is rinsed with the only substance pure enough to prepare the bottle, Absolut itself.

We could practically say the line in our sleep. But could a campaign be built around one factoid? While the clients were uniformly behind the idea, Persson insisted we come up with two dozen (!) nuggets before they would agree to proceed. There just had to be others. So Joey, Andy, and Neal Davies journeyed to Drakamöllan, Sweden, to spend a day in a charming farmhouse, nugget-hunting with Absolut staffers. Unfortunately, Sweden was playing Argentina in the World Cup, so the meeting was pushed back one day. (Nuggets are nuggets but soccer is SOCCER.)

Meanwhile, Joey had fingered Irving Penn to do the photography. When it turned out that Penn was unavailable, Joey selected the husband-wife team of Coppi-Barbieri.

Fabrizio Coppi and Lucille Barbieri are an Italian couple living in London. Joey's enthusiasm was contagious, so an agreement was quickly reached. "These would be portraits of the bottle as if it were human. And they would be two-page spreads, so you might say they were big humans."

Andy Hall had attended divinity school prior to entering advertising. He was to some extent still under the influence. He penned the campaign's tagline, "Our devotion to perfection is Absolut." And he meant it. In fact, nearly all the headlines took on a heavenly froth.

REGRETS

chapter nine

JE NE REGRET RIEN. WELL, MAYBE. I DON'T HAVE MANY REGRETS. MORE SPECIFICALLY,

ABSOLUT REGRETS. However, in order to make this book more entertaining I want to

devote a chapter to two kinds of Absolut ads: those I wished we DID and, the natural

counterpart, those I wished we DIDN'T.

Obviously, this is a bit of a stepchild to the "Rejects" chapter I included in the ABSOLUT BOOK. There, though, the purpose was to assemble a few dozen ads that had been rejected by the Absolut clients. I purposely included some that were laughably bad to reinforce the notion that the Agency wasn't always right, either. Neither my heart nor my mind were exactly upset when they didn't get to the printer.

WE WISH WE DID

The "Wish We Did" ads are different. I wanted them to happen but they didn't. They stumbled and fell for any of many reasons: they may not even have made it to a presentation; OR they were rejected by one or more clients; OR the necessary talent, artist, or partner wouldn't cooperate; OR some other advertiser did an ad that was uncomfortably similar so we killed it; OR it just cost too much to make.

ABSOLUT SUCKS First on everyone's list. SUCKS was a great eye-twister because Absolut doesn't suck. But it's not afraid to pretend to. This Dan Braun creation required a real act of client bravery (or stupidity, if you listened to its detractors). Goran Lundqvist loved the ad but wouldn't force Seagram to do it. It was re-presented at so many meetings the client was surprised—and relieved—when we finally didn't show it.

ABSOLUT ENTREPRENEUR Another Dan Brauny creation. ENTREPRENEUR was "squelched" because the Seagram lawyers felt it was too reminiscent of kids' lemonade stands. But that was exactly the point.

ABSOLUT SACRIFICE Great Absolut Citron ads were scarce. And in my mind, a lemon has no more noble calling than to be squeezed, wrung, dehydrated and ultimately sacrificed to help create a bottle of Citron. Obviously, I got carried away in my enthusiasm, which surely helped to un-sell this Simon McQuoid and Richard Overall idea.

ABSOLUT SESSION I always felt we didn't have enough ads in our unofficial "therapy" series (AROMATHERAPY, YOGA, RELAXATION, etc.). So when we came up with this Ode to Freud, I believed we were also saluting the branch of medicine that is also complicit in satirizing itself, psychiatry.

ABSOLUT LEVITTOWN One didn't have to actually be raised in Levittown to feel its impact. This Long Island, New York burg became famous because a builder, Bill Levitt, spawned a pilgrimage to suburbia by creating simple (two bedroom, one bath), affordable (below $8,000), but cookie-cutter housing in the 1940s. If he were alive today he wouldn't recognize the place: nearly every homeowner subsequently customized the homes to fit their own taste.

ABSOLUT JOKE This idea is surely in the "SUCKS" family. We were poking fun at the proliferation of the shelf-stable, non-refrigerated juice box packaging that arose in the 90s. We asked, what would it look like if a juice box package was combined with Absolut's iconic bottle design? While it didn't meet the client's standards for a "real" ad, it did actually appear once in a publication of rejected ads.

ABSOLUT KEROUAC This is another minor masterpiece from Nandi Ahuja, the Merrill Lynch banker who really just wants to be a poor, suffering adman.

ABSOLUT CITRON These two ideas come from our failed "Yellow Surprise" campaign for Citron. We tried, sometimes desperately, to shoot every lemon- or lime-related idea in sight. Carl, unfortunately, was never a big insect guy. In fact, I was once with him in Stockholm when a bee stung him. He wasn't happy. As for the monkeys idea, you may draw your own conclusions.

WE WISH WE DIDN'T

Now, the Didn't. Sometimes in advertising, as in life, ideas turn sour. It's not like an idea looks great on Tuesday but terrible by Thursday. Of course, that happens, too. I'm referring to ideas that get stale after a lengthy approval, production, or publication process. By the time they actually appear, we may be scratching our heads, wondering, "What were we thinking?" And sometimes the execution just doesn't live up to the vision. As Joey says, "You can't always build it." And sometimes, even great clients ask you to do dumb things.

All these ads appeared at least once in real magazines. May the advertising gods forgive us.

ABSOLUT CITRON (ZEST) This ad is everyone's favorite least favorite. It was supposed to be a delicate lemon peeler, with the zest creating the bottle shape. The result was quite different: a grotesque cheese grater. This patient had numerous visits to the advertising ER, where we should have kindly let it die.

ABSOLUT UPGRADE The best thing I can say about this ad is there are no typos. It's all status: welcome to first-class snobbery. There's no wink, no humor, no smile. And aren't we cute? We included another Absolut ad in the passenger's magazine. We just overindulged at the "Take Yourself Seriously" bar.

ABSOLUT 24ᵀᴴ I love the guys who did this ad—Simon

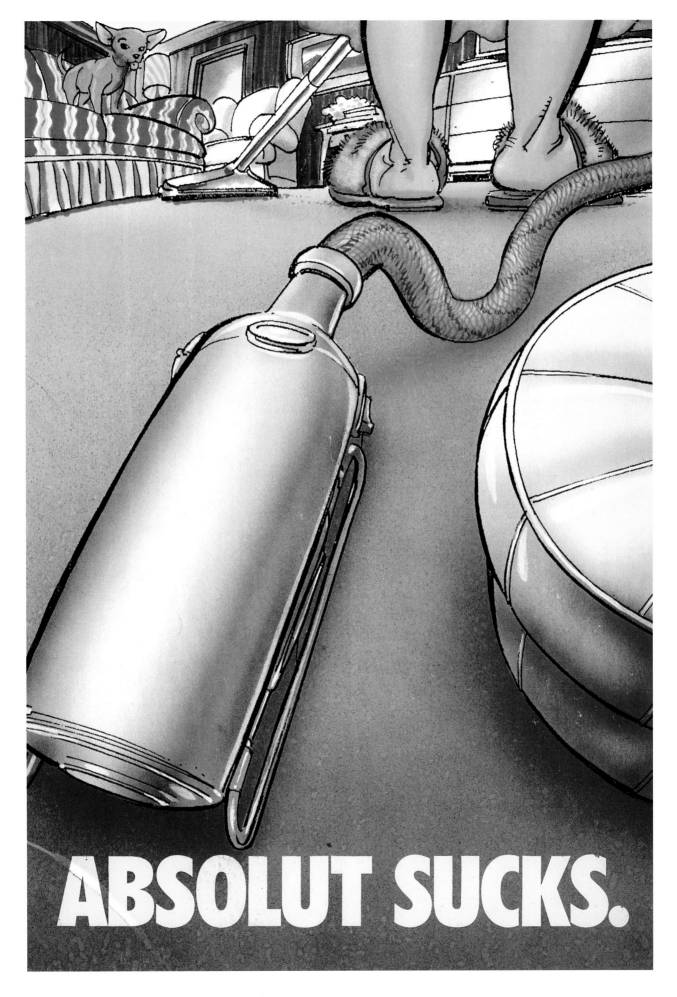

ABSOLUT SESSION.

ABSOLUT LEVITTOWN.

ABSOLUT CITRON.

ABSOLUT CITRON.

ABSOLUT JOKE.

ABSOLUT CITRON.

ABSOLUT UPGRADE.

ABSOLUT 24TH.

ABSOLUT LATEST.

ABSOLUT MIX.

McQuoid and Rich Overall. They're annoying perfection-ists when they're not just plain old fun. But this salute to the excesses of holiday shopping is not in the Absolut spirit. Not to mention, the woman should've changed her shoes when it started to snow.

ABSOLUT LATEST and **ABSOLUT MIX** These are two differ-ent ads that are joined at the cool hip. In part, Absolut became lovable because it poked fun at the conventionally cool. Here, mistakenly, we openly embrace it. LATEST is a little less annoying because it's supposed to be an over-the-top PDA, but it just doesn't work. MIX wasn't just a bad idea—saluting the deejay life—it was also hard on the eyes.

ABSOLUT VINTAGE and **ABSOLUT LEGACY** This might be the dumbest idea we ever had: Let's highlight, literally, the important words on the bottle so people get the points . . . we're old, Swedish, and tasty. By the way, I promised Dan Braun I wouldn't tell anyone this was his brainchild, so please keep it a secret.

SPUMONI

chapter ten

FORGIVE ME FOR THE TITLE. I HAVE ITALIAN DESSERTS ON THE BRAIN.
This past weekend, Memorial Day, 2004, I was having dinner with my son Sam at a restaurant—coincidentally, called Sam's—in the village where we live. At dessert time, the waiter was racing through the selections when he came to spumoni, tortoni, and tartufo. I embarrassedly confessed to Sam that his fifty-something Dad still didn't know the difference between all these multiflavored ice cream treats and probably never would get it straight. The waiter, patiently, took us through a detailed description of each—"It's got some chocolate, I see some strawberry, maybe a little vanilla, some cherries, too, it's very cold"—but I'd be damned if I could tell you forty-eight hours later what's what. Anyway, my Sam just wanted a cannoli, which they didn't have, so he passed on dessert.

Which calls to mind the staggering number of choices consumers face in the flavored-vodka business. Ten years ago I could count every flavored vodka in the USA on the fingers of my two hands. Stoli had pepper, lemon, orange, and a wacky honey-hunter flavor. Absolut had pepper (Peppar), lemon (Citron), and currant (Kurant). And that was about it. But in the past decade there's been nothing short of a flavor explosion—with every established and wannabe vodka in every price segment participating.

I'm not exaggerating. First, I don't have to, and second, because my friend Jim Schleiffer, Absolut's VP/Sales in the States, will confirm that nearly 500 different flavored vodkas have been introduced.

The flavored vodka epidemic has gone way beyond the traditional citrus flavors. Nearly every fruit is represented. (Though I'm still waiting for my banana.) Like Baskin-Robbins, there's vanilla, chocolate, and strawberry; not to mention coffee, grapefruit, and various spice combinations. The vodka market isn't all that different from most other consumer categories in the U.S. market. (Well, hopefully the consumers are a little older.)

When I was growing up, for example, there was only one type of Cheerios: regular round, crunchy oats. Now there's frosted, honey-nut, multigrain, apple-cinnamon, and a mixed version of most of those varieties, plus three versions with berries and bananas. (You're welcome, General Mills.) And, surely, you've noticed what's happened to Oreos. There must be twenty varieties including "Uh-Oh," which flips the standard chocolate cookie/vanilla filling on its head.

The reasons for this aren't very complicated. Every now and then, consumers need a break from their everyday tipple. They can get it by trying a fashionable new cocktail or a new product or both. If they already enjoy vodka and are loyal to a particular brand, the choice is easy—if that brand offers them something new: a new taste, but with the same price and quality and a similar connection to the brand.

Marketers love this kind of brand "extension," too. They can keep a customer in the "family," can participate in a growing market, and can do so on the back of the existing brand machine. The alternative is to literally start from scratch with every product, which is always more expensive and much riskier. Of course, a marketer cannot extend a brand forever, but it's fun and profitable until you reach the end of the road.

It has always been a challenge to do flavor advertising as tasty as the flavored vodka, particularly as we have been try-ing to communicate the flavor "story" in every ad. Great ABSOLUT CITRON ads have always been tough to do — they come with a lemon ball and chain attached. We flirted with the color yellow as an alternative communication device (sorry for the jargon), but that proved to be hit or miss, with a lousy batting average. We thought we had a hit—and an idea—with the taxi ad. The concept even had a name: Yellow Surprise. This confluence of yellow objects looked great downtown. Elsewhere it proved to be a struggle. The "Oasis" ad was so parched no number of flowers could save it. And the ad we called "Butterflies" Carl Horton called "Moths"; it deserved its nickname.

These ads were also hobbled because they all carried the ABSOLUT CITRON headline. We couldn't use the traditional two-word approach, because the ads didn't show actual bottles. Without ABSOLUT CITRON, how would consumers know whether we were advertising CITRON or ABSOLUT BLUE (aka Absolut vodka)?

There was no interplay between word and picture, which is a campaign hallmark. Not to mention, it was very confusing to us, too. If every ad had the same headline, they needed a nickname, so that we could tell them apart. And you thought this was Easy Street?

MANDRIN

Since Absolut doesn't introduce and withdraw flavors like Baskin-Robbins, a new product is a major event. When ABSOLUT MANDRIN was born in 1999, it was the first introduction in seven years.

As Carl Horton so often said, "No one's waiting for Absolut to introduce an orange vodka." Given that Stoli had introduced their very successful Stoli Ohranj (or Stoli O as it came to be called) a full five years earlier, Absolut had to significantly differentiate its version.

Eva Kempe-Forsberg had arrived at Absolut the year before. She was hired by marketing director Lars Nellmer to head new products. Previously, Eva had been marketing director at Henkel Cosmetics. Eva is soft spoken, contemplative, and passionate about all things Absolut, and was also clearly self-assured. While she didn't relish tangling with the noisy Americans, us included, she wasn't afraid to, either.

Working with Pearlfisher, a London design consultancy, Eva was like a silk-padded battering ram. Over months of cantankerous meetings over the product name, composition, and bottle design, Eva pulled everyone together from

ABSOLUT SIGHTING.

ABSOLUT ARRIVAL.

ABSOLUT BALANCE.

ABSOLUT SQUEEZE.

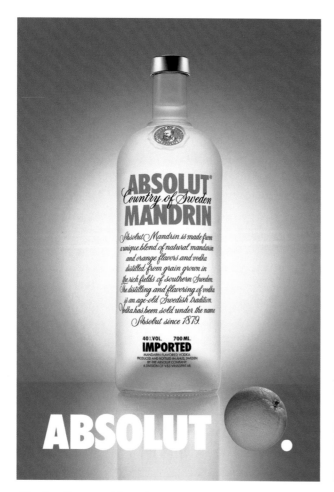

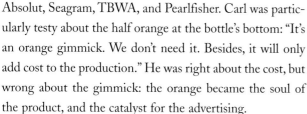

Absolut, Seagram, TBWA, and Pearlfisher. Carl was particularly testy about the half orange at the bottle's bottom: "It's an orange gimmick. We don't need it. Besides, it will only add cost to the production." He was right about the cost, but wrong about the gimmick: the orange became the soul of the product, and the catalyst for the advertising.

Bob Kuperman was now the TBWA\Chiat\Day creative director in New York—because he had fired practically everyone else. Kuperman, something of a legend in the ad business for possessing a mix of talent and temper, was an art director from the Doyle Dane Bernbach heyday in the 1960s. He then hooked up with Jay Chiat in 1987, and rose to become Chiat/Day's president at the time of the 1995 merger with TBWA.

The Agency had recently moved back to midtown after two and a half years in a playpen purgatory—the infamous Chiat/Day office-less office—downtown on Maiden Lane. This would be Kuperman's first creative leadership for Absolut and first dance with Carl Horton.

After a slew of false starts, including a sleepy trip to the Orient incorporating Asian imagery, we arrived at a positioning best described as the "King of Oranges." While hardly a startling idea, it did fit with Mandrin's taste complexity and the stunning bottle design. The

actual orange was going to be the flavor's vehicle: we would pluck it from outer space and land it inside the bottle. It would be juicy, tantalizing, fresh, and ripe for hero status. The orange was ready for its close-up.

"Nobody eats or drinks blue products. Why does the background have to be blue?" Sometimes, Carl got right to the heart of the matter. There weren't any blue edibles or potables five years ago. (Since then, however, there's been a blue epidemic: Gatorade (Fierce and Frost), M&M's, Kool-Aid, Jell-O, Betty Crocker Fruit Gushers, Hypnotiq liqueur, and Magellan Gin. To name but a few.) But that wasn't the point. The blue was there to make the orange orange-r—as blue is orange's opposite on the color wheel. You could see the smoke coming out of Kuperman's ears. Blue smoke as I remember. He challenged Carl to show the ads to consumers. I'm thinking, no, that's a terrible idea; Carl might say yes. We had survived up to now by keeping consumers out of the advertising kitchen. Carl said he would think about it, but we could tell he wouldn't. He didn't care about setting a research precedent. He was worried the consumers would tell him he was wrong. So blue it was and blue it is. But that was the first and last meeting for Kuperman & Horton. They were just too flammable a combination.

ABSOLUT CLICHÉ Would it have read better as ABSOLUT APHORISM? Or ABSOLUT SAYING? Or ABSOLUT EXPRESSION? In the end, "cliché" was the best choice, as the alternatives were like comparing apples to oranges.

ABSOLUT ● This was the first (and last) example of an Absolut headline that employed a picture of a fruit instead of a word. The working name was Kramer, as in Seinfeld's Cosmo Kramer. You might ask why? Because that's how Kramer would deliver that orange right onto the page with a POP! sound and wild, waving, arm motion.

ABSOLUT FENG SHUI and **ABSOLUT SIESTA** Both these ads were actually hatched for Absolut vodka. But as we had a surplus of BLUE ads and a shortage of ORANGE ads, we asked, "Why can't they apply for a transfer?" Aside from the obvious conclusion that we could come up with only so many orange-inspired "observations," we reasoned that the flavors deserved some better thinking, certainly some better headlines. I was a big proponent of this logic; so if you disagree, blame me.

Mandrin was a hit from the start. As Absolut introduced new flavors so infrequently, apparently people were eagerly awaiting the new Absolut. The launch was so successful that distributors pleaded with the Swedes to keep the factory open during the month of July as opposed to its annual closing for employee vacations. (It remained closed.)

However, by 2002, the same distributors were moaning that sales were slowing because "consumers didn't know how to drink" Mandrin. The Agency had gotten away scot-free, for years, from having to develop what are known as "recipe" ads, because we were convinced consumers had other ways to find out—at bars, from friends, or the media. Here was another way for Absolut to stand out: No dopey recipe ads.

The pressure was unremitting. Patrick O'Neill was committed to making the best of it. He engineered a campaign he called "+." The objective was to communicate how Absolut makes every cocktail better. The visual idea was a severe close-up of the drink. You would be so close, you wouldn't see the glass, just the liquid. The effect is something similar to staring into an aquarium or fish-tank—without the fish. If you ask Patrick today what he thinks of the ads, he's sorry he didn't put his head in the aquarium instead. The magazine ads could slide into the "Wish We Didn't Do" department. But the outdoor work, particularly the building wraps, was actually striking.

VANILIA

Most of 2002 was spent developing Absolut Vanilia. It was clear at Absolut that new products needed a higher priority and a faster track. Their new president, Bengt Baron, began to light fires. Bengt succeeded Goran Lundqvist, who retired in a departure worthy of the Queen of England. Goran was a beloved people-person at Vin & Sprit, Absolut's Swedish parent company, and from that standpoint he would be a difficult act to follow.

But Bengt is no shrinking violet either. Like Lundqvist, he was an Olympic athlete, winning a silver medal for swimming during the 1988 Tokyo Olympics. His business career included stints at Kodak, Coca Cola, and McKinsey. This might be his first foray into spirits, but he knew consumer goods. And he recognized that as proud and close-knit as the Absolut culture was, the company and the brand needed an injection of new spirit.

Introducing a vanilla-flavored vodka in a marketplace that already had three vanillas (Stoli, Skyy, and Smirnoff) would require an Absolut edge. Fortunately, it had one: its proof. The competitors' vanillas were 70 proof (35 percent alcohol) while Absolut Vanilia, like its sister flavors, was 80 proof. This was a difference Absolut had never emphasized before. Now it would. Because the proof difference clearly produced a taste difference. So it was time to sprinkle our magic dust.

Neal Davies was the sprinkler. Neal arrived at TBWA\Chiat\Day in New York during the English invasion of 1999–2000. Neal was an account director at our London office, working on Sony PlayStation. When his boss, Carl Johnson, became the New York office president, he invited Neal and most of Manchester United to join him and stir things up. Neal is a great character. Now in his mid thirties, he's immodestly ambitious, highly energized, fun, and either knows something about everything or can find out in an instant. He was also a real Americaphile, and knew the history of the New York Mets better than I did. Plus he designed and wrote great PowerPoint presentations, which aren't my strong suit. So when he joined our group there was plenty for him to do.

Neal used the Absolut difference in the proof to create, what, in effect, became the flavor's position, "Rich, robust, and complex. It's a different kind of Vanilla." Hmmm: he took a sleepy, bland flavor (think "plain vanilla"), one that was preferred by women, and gave it a macho posture suitable for men in bars. And it worked. The creatives used

ABSOLUT EXTRACT.

RICH, ROBUST, AND COMPLEX. IT'S A DIFFERENT KIND OF VANILLA.

this position to design ads that made vanilla a killa.

ABSOLUT EXTRACT We kicked off the Vanilia campaign with an old-fashioned print spectacular. Readers could pop-out, or literally extract, this replica of the beautiful new Absolut bottle, and post it as a prominent reminder to buy the real McCoy the next time they got to the store.

ABSOLUT HEAVYWEIGHT and **ABSOLUT PERSISTENCE** These two ads made it abundantly clear that Absolut Vanilia wasn't your typical wimpy vanilla: it could crush spoons and ice cream cones. So stay away if you're only man enough for your sister's vanilla.

ABSOLUT AWE I've always had a heart for cookies that can emote, and this ad, with its saluting vanilla wafers, is my favorite. Smooch.

RASPBERRI

The theme for the 2004 Raspberri launch was "Unleash the Raspberry." Like vanilla, the objective was to give the normally sweet but mousy berry a tougher personality. "Because raspberries are so cute, they're often underesti-

mated in the fruit department," believes Patrick O'Neill. "They have a certain moxie to them Absolut tapped into that's in the liquid and that we wanted to be sure found its way into the advertising."

In an Art Guys–type update, O'Neill led the creative team of Lauren Harwell and Gail Barlow, who were interested in not simply painting interpretations of the bottle, but painting the bottle itself.

ABSOLUT RELEASE New York artists from the Barnstormers—Maya Hayuk and Kenji Hirata, plus Phil Frost, took turns painting the crimson red Absolut Raspberri bottle while Barnstormer David Ellis, aka Squirm, filmed each artist at work. (Between painters, the bottle was scrubbed and dried for its next performance. Before they could even get to know their babies, they were gone.) But these films were cut to thirty-second television spots, a first for the brand, so their images will live on.

And did consumers razz the personality uplift from this humble berry? Not at all: they, too, were waiting for Absolut to put its stamp on this flavor.

ABSOLUT PROPS SHOT

THE MASTER BUILDERS AT MCCONNELL & BOROW HAVE BEEN CREATING the bottle props since before the flood. At a recent prop reunion we encouraged many of the attendees to assemble for a group shot. In case you have difficulty identifying any of the actors:

Sort of the front row (l-r):

KILLINGTON, KARLOFF, SADIST, MARILYN, SHELLY, STANDARD

Kind of the back row:

MORPH, PITTSBURGH, RINGER, APPEAL, REVEAL, TEXAS, CITRON

ABSOLUT ORIGIN

ANNY ANNIE

chapter eleven

WHEN ABSOLUT WAS ON THE VERGE OF TURNING TWENTY BACK IN 2000, we wanted to come up with an appropriate way to celebrate the anniversary. As the brand had debuted in the USA in 1979, selling the first bottles in Boston, we would actually be celebrating the twentieth anniversary of the advertising in 2000. While it may appear to be self-serving for the advertising agency to recommend such recognition for the advertising (and agencies are always accused of self-serving behavior, most of it deserved), it was actually the Absolut clients who pushed the idea.

One of the great freedoms of anniversaries like these is that nobody other than the celebrants knows the "real" anniversary, so we had a great deal of latitude in deciding when to celebrate. So we picked June 2000. It gave us six months to get ready and then six months to celebrate. That sounded like a proper ratio. (An example of an improper ratio is a sixty-minute wait for a two-minute ride on Space Mountain at Disney World.)

Our first idea was to do another one of our modestly titled print "spectaculars." The brand had become famous for manufacturing talking and singing ads, snow-globes, stockings, scarves, and gloves, all delivered in magazines.

One early idea had been a wristwatch that would count down to the millennium. Another was to throw an Absolut party in some stadium, distributing the tickets in random copies of *Entertainment Weekly*. (That idea quickly got bogged down in party logistics.)

An early favorite of mine was a four-page ad of 500 Absolut stickers, each one representing a different Absolut ad. The kicker was there would be one ringer, one Absolut ad that was a phony. Readers would then be invited to find the ringer and mail it in, for the chance to win a trip to Sweden—of course. In fact, I distinctly remember presenting the idea and a full comp at a Stockholm meeting. While we were debating the pluses and minuses, one of the Seagram clients, Drew DeSarno, a good-natured guy with an abundance of patience, spent a half hour looking for the fake ad. When he gave up and cried "uncle," I persuaded him to try once more. He did, but still couldn't find it. "What's with these guys?" I thought. I didn't want to let him off the hook. Finally, I took the comp back, giving it a quick once-over, and I realized we forgot to put in the phony ad. Oops. Anyway, back in New York, the idea didn't get past the Seagram lawyers. They insisted that stickers were the provenance of kids (maybe even using that word), so the ad was dead. Joey Mazzaferro said it was probably for the better; the anniversary deserved something more special. Typically for Joey, he had already hatched that more special idea.

Annie Leibovitz is the nonpareil celebrity photographer in America. Since her start at *Rolling Stone* in the 1970s, moving on to *Vanity Fair* in the 1980s, Leibovitz has photographed presidents, kings, Hollywood, and athletes. She began with the rock 'n' roll elite, including Mick Jagger, Jim Morrison, and John Lennon. She's always had the uncanny ability of not just capturing her subjects' beauty or power or electricity but also transforming them into even greater gods than they already are. Leibovitz is a contemporary version of one of those seventeenth-century masters—like Caravaggio—who painted royalty to guarantee their immortality.

We were introduced through our friends at *Vanity Fair*, particularly, Peter King Hunsinger, who was publisher at the time, and a very classy guy all the time. Peter warned me, "She's a little tough to work with." Annie does this all for a price. Plenty of money, of course, but much more: total and utter creative control.

Joey's idea was to have Annie shoot twenty interesting people, each posed with their favorite Absolut ad from the previous twenty years. A simple and elegant idea. What Joey and the rest of us didn't realize until the train left the station was that Annie had to choose or approve all the people, the ads, the shots' props, even the people she would permit into her studio to watch her shoot. Did I mention she was also pretty insistent on what fruits the caterer set out on the plates?

If I appear to be griping, I'm not. This project never would have happened without Leibovitz. Like a queen bee magnet, her name could attract the talent. And while there were obviously people who declined, I had the sense that everyone asked actually considered participating. Leibovitz and her Praetorian Guard led by her agent, Jim Moffat, pulled it off. Incidentally, everyone who appeared in the ad was paid the same fee; and most of the fees were donated to their favorite charities. Remember, we're doing vodka advertising here, albeit great vodka and pretty good advertising.

Leibovitz also has to be credited for each portrait's composition, how she incorporated the Absolut ad without it overwhelming the portrait. For instance, if I had been the photographer, everyone would probably have been positioned in the same way: standing, from the chest up, like a mug shot. She was a lot more original. Many of the ads are barely visible. Some appear within a pile on the floor. Others are being stepped on, both shoed and shoeless, rolled up, or in their natural habitat, within the covers of a magazine.

RUSHDIE The challenge was to get a tasty bouillabaisse of personalities, particularly from the arts. We also wanted a firecracker. Al Sharpton said yes but we said no. Too bad: he would've raised the edginess a notch. But Salman Rushdie certainly did that. Five years ago, Rushdie was still under a fatwa, a death sentence from Iran, for writing *The Satanic Verses*, a Nobel Prize–winning parable that offended the Muslim clerics. Rushdie spent a decade, virtually in

TOM FORD.

CHUCK CLOSE.

HELMUT NEWTON.

SALMAN RUSHDIE.

JERRY LEWIS.

GUS VAN SANT.

hiding, under the protection of the British government—he's a British subject—until the fatwa was unofficially lifted in 1998. Bookstores around the world, including many in the USA, refused to carry the book for fear of Islamic reprisals. Rushdie was photographed holding a copy of ABSOLUT ORIGINAL. The ad is aflame; his eyes are bloodshot and weary.

LEWIS On the other end of the cultural funnel there's Jerry Lewis (no relation). Lewis appears with a water glass in his mouth (and I mean, in his mouth), wearing a serious expression and a cut-out bottle from ABSOLUT LAS VEGAS (with the sticker that reads: "Hello. My name is Absolut.") This was his idea, while vamping for the camera. I've been a Jerry Lewis fan since I was a kid (check out *The Absent-Minded Professor*), so I introduced myself at the shoot. We acknowledged that neither one of our names is really "Lewis." (He was born Joseph Levitch.)

The twentieth anniversary was officially celebrated on June 7, 2000. A fortnight-long exhibition of Absolut art was arranged in Vanderbilt Hall at New York's Grand Central Station, and was visited by 12,000 people over two weeks. Annie Leibovitz didn't attend the party, but Salman Rushdie did.

ABSOLUT DAD.

ABSOLUT DAD

This one-of-a-kind ad deserves its own page! ABSOLUT DAD ran just once on Father's Day, June 1997. This ode to Dad included the archetype Father's Day gift: the necktie. What set this tie apart was not just the fact it couldn't be returned to Macy's. But the presence of the sperm-shaped Absolut bottles, the origin of all fathers. And mothers. Regis Philbin wore the tie on his show the following day.

JUMP THE NET

chapter twelve

WHAT SEEMS LIKE AT LEAST TEN YEARS AGO, BUT MAY HAVE BEEN AS FEW AS FIVE, my wife Isabel came home with a story. Isabel is a recruiter, or what is more typically called a headhunter. She gets people jobs. Her specialty is law firms. Not lawyers, but everyone else: legal secretaries, paralegals, office managers. Isabel has been doing this forever; in fact, that's how we met. I had a brief and very unsuccessful fling in the personnel business way back when. As bad as I was, she's that good.

```
..............absolutvodka.com..............
........launches an experiment in...........
......interactive        communication.....
.................over    the................
.................web.    The................
...............site      invites............
............users        to explore.........
...........a space       of art and.........
.........ideas,          evolving..........
.........out of          a unifying........
........theme.           Each.............
.....edition             will be..........
....refreshed            daily,..........
....with new             themes...........
....emerging             periodically...
.........Our             first...........
.....edition,            Absolut Kelly,..
.........seeks           the emergent...
.......wisdom            of the..........
.......whole,            by drawing.....
.....a single            outcome........
.....from                the many.......
.....voices              of the.........
.........net.            The site.......
.....is tuned            for the........
............Netscape browser.............
```

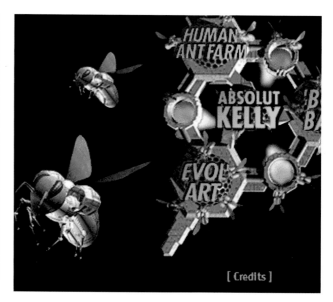

[Credits]

Isabel meets a lot of characters in the course of her work, and she often regales us with stories about these people's lives, at least to the extent they intersect with hers. Anyway, she came home one night and told the assembled family that she had an odd applicant that day. For the sake of this story, let's call her Sharon. Sharon was an individual who had no marketable skills. She had no work experience in an office. She couldn't type. And she appeared a little aimless. Isabel, getting desperate, asked, "What do you like to do?" To which Sharon replied, "I surf the Net." Isabel, without missing a beat, asked, "What net?"

What net indeed? A real decade ago, at TBWA, we were trying to wrestle this bear to the ground—to figure out how Absolut would appear—and behave—on the Internet. Pete Callaro, the Absolut A. E., my bear cub at the Agency, was fascinated and became a missionary and proselytizer for the World Wide Web. Pete had joined the Agency directly out of Rutgers University in 1990. Everyone liked him. He had brains, manners, and good looks. I remember my boss, Bill Tragos, warning me, "Don't turn him into a wise-ass like you, Lewis." Too late, that was also in Pete's blood.

Pete educated the clients and the Agency about the great adventure just beginning in cyberspace, and what it would mean to advertising. I recall sitting in all these presentations, wondering, what was he talking about? And appreciating that I didn't have to know because he did. Pete convinced everyone that the Web was a must-do for the brand; he also convinced everyone that the must-not-do was to simply put the Absolut campaign on the Web. He reasoned, this wasn't just another static medium like outdoor or print. And before anyone had converted to convergence, Pete declared the Web was going to do it all: words, pictures, sounds, info, art,

emotion, and maybe even G-d. At least, that's how I remember it today. The crazy thing wasn't that we all listened to him, but that he was almost right.

We embarked on a series of adventures that were targeted at the Web pioneers, the experimenters, the digerati, the Web denizens. We identified two groups. The first group was composed of the "rad-grads." They were designing and building the technological innovations driving the Internet: jpegs, video-streaming, and flash; the tools that made multimedia multi. Many had been playing with computers since they were kids, and college had just been one big laboratory. The second group, the digital paparazzi, was writing and chronicling the exploits of the rad-grads. *Wired* magazine was their bible. As Absolut was a cutting-edge brand in the arts, it would also endeavor to be that brand on the Web. This meant we would use the constantly expanding palette of Web tools to not just create our sites, but to promote, even require, interactivity from the visitors. This was pretty heady stuff in 1995—when our competitors were largely content with launching drink recipes into cyberspace.

ABSOLUT KELLY With our typical modesty, we titled this the "Visionary" series. Callaro posed the question, "What would be the result if we paired Frank Zappa and Nostradamus? Albert Einstein and Madonna? Casey Stengel and Woodrow Wilson? We enlisted *Wired* editor Kevin Kelly to be our travel agent. Kelly had recently written *Out of Control*, a book that explored the marriage of technology and biology. One possible result: robot bees, which became the mascots of the Web site. Kelly's thinking was, if computers, whose DNA is digital, could get viruses, why couldn't insects?

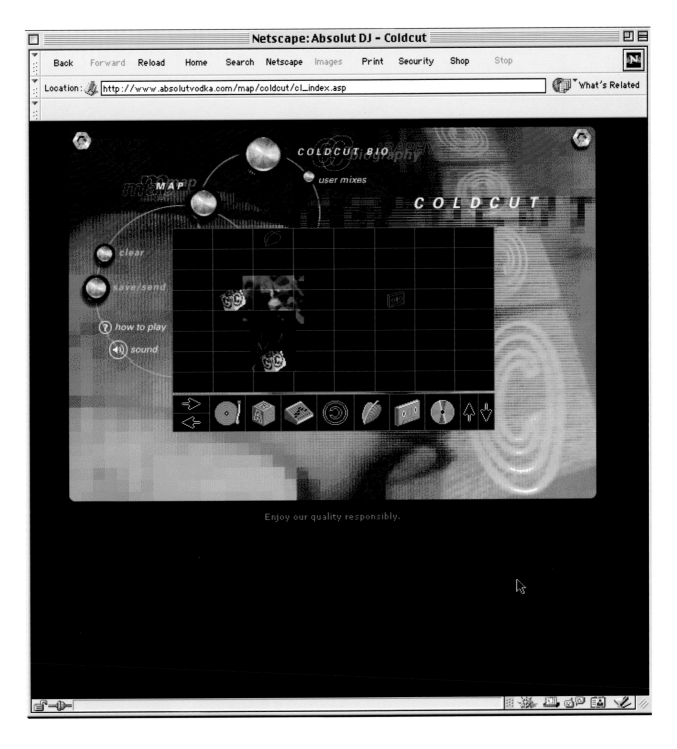

But everyone's favorite part of the site had to be the "Human Ant Farm." In a storefront in Santa Monica, California, we parked artists such as Kenny Scharf to paint inside the street window. A minicam followed his every move. Visitors could determine what stimuli he was exposed to: the type of music he would hear (reggae, rock, New Age); the food he could eat (dim sum, carrot juice, Tandoori chicken); the lights he would labor under (strobe, candles, or fluorescents). And then we could continuously track the progress of the art. (Kenny Scharf would be the first to tell you that Nabisco Honey

Grahams are a great catalyst.) Another popular feature was "EvoArt," a community location that enabled visitors to continuously create and alter the art of other site visitors through the use of a computer graphic interface. Pete dubbed it "Democratic Art."

ABSOLUT PANUSHKA ABSOLUT PANUSHKA was born the following year. Christine Panushka was the dean of the Animation Department at Cal Arts in Pasadena. Pete, collaborating with Debra Calabrese at Troon, an Internet content factory in Los Angeles, headed up by Chris Tragos, came up with the idea of creating little Absolut animations

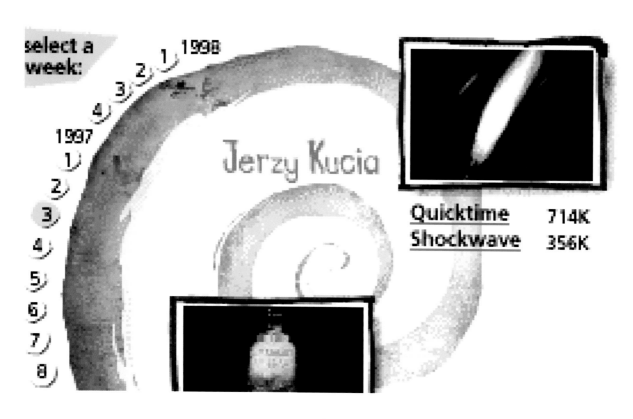

for the Web. Panushka, using her queen bee powers, invited nearly three dozen leading animators to join in. Essentially an extension of the Absolut artist campaign, the site also included an historic timeline of film animation.

ABSOLUT DJ By now, the Web had become so popular, it was overrun with grandmothers. In 1998, Absolut recognized the growing interest in the underground mixes and sampling of DJs. The idea, here, was to create "visual music" so it could be gently branded with Absolut bottles. Working with Kirk Gibbons of RedSky, who created the visuals, the site featured the music of Coldcut, DJ Spooky, UFO, and Riz Mazlen. Visitors could make their own mixes on an interactive keyboard and then e-mail them to their friends.

ABSOLUT TINY FILMS

Simon McQuoid and Richard Overall are two Aussies (Australians, that is) who came to the USA fifteen years ago. Simon (the art director) and Richard (the writer) have worked together and separately at a few agencies. They

arrived separately at TBWA in 1999, Simon believes. In fact, he even was a little uncertain about who hired him, not because it was anything approaching a secret but because the creative directors were "coming and going like express trains at rush hour."

Like all the Agency's creative teams, they were drafted for the annual Absolut presentation of 2000. As Simon recalls, "there were loads and loads of great print ads in the mix. Perhaps we should do something different." They came up with the idea of TV spots for the Internet. These would be short—ten-second—spots that would be original Absolut "bottle" ads. But they would also be little stories with action and sound. One Tuesday afternoon they wrote six scripts and then produced them as QuickTime movies, with a minimum of props, in the Agency that evening. They're witty, light, and irreverent; they're very Absolut.

ABSOLUT LOS ANGELES For instance: Open to show a bottle. A dog barks. The bottle shakes and vibrates. Car horns honk. Headline appears: ABSOLUT LOS ANGELES. It's just another L.A. earthquake.

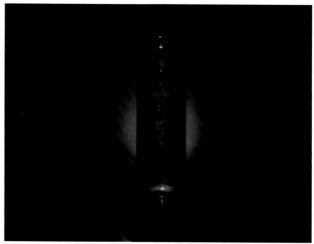

ABSOLUT MYSTERY Or: Open to show a bottle. Sound of electric sizzle. Lights out. A punch and a fall. Woman screams. Lights back on to reveal bottle on its side, stabbed with a kitchen knife. Sound of thunder. Headline appears: ABSOLUT MYSTERY.

ONLINE FEVER

In 2001, Doug Jaeger was a hotshot at the digital division of J. Walter Thompson, working on significant clients such as Merrill Lynch and DeBeers. His work caught the attention of TBWA president Carl Johnson, who said, "Let's get him." Doug thought he was happy at JWT, so he resisted the TBWA magnet. But we had an idea that proved irresistible: we would buy "his" URL, dougjaeger.com, preventing him from using his own name on the Web, something that would surely drive him crazy. And did. He signed up right away. "When I arrived, there was a punch list of projects for nearly every client. It was a little overwhelming." And it takes a lot to overwhelm Doug, a voluble, self-confident, 24/7 idea person. A wall of account people could give him a resounding "No." Without missing a beat, he'd ask, "Well, what about this other idea?"

We were always trying to figure out what was next for Absolut. While we were continuing the Visionary series, it also was apparent it was time for some actual advertising on the Web. The Agency certainly had the Internet fever. Nearly every department was staffed with newly minted dot-commers.

This was the brainchild of Nick McLean, a brilliant but a little loony media director and strategist. McLean was part

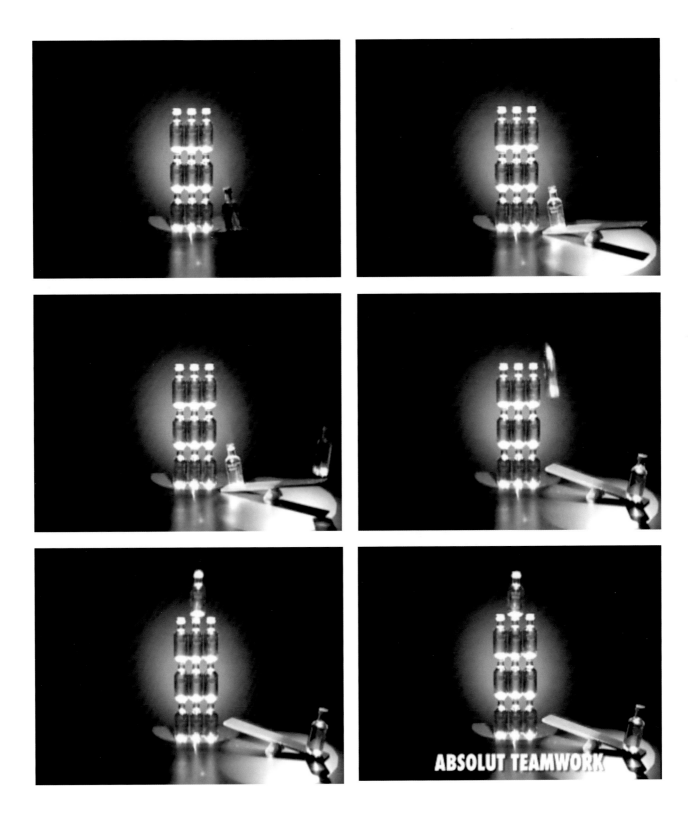

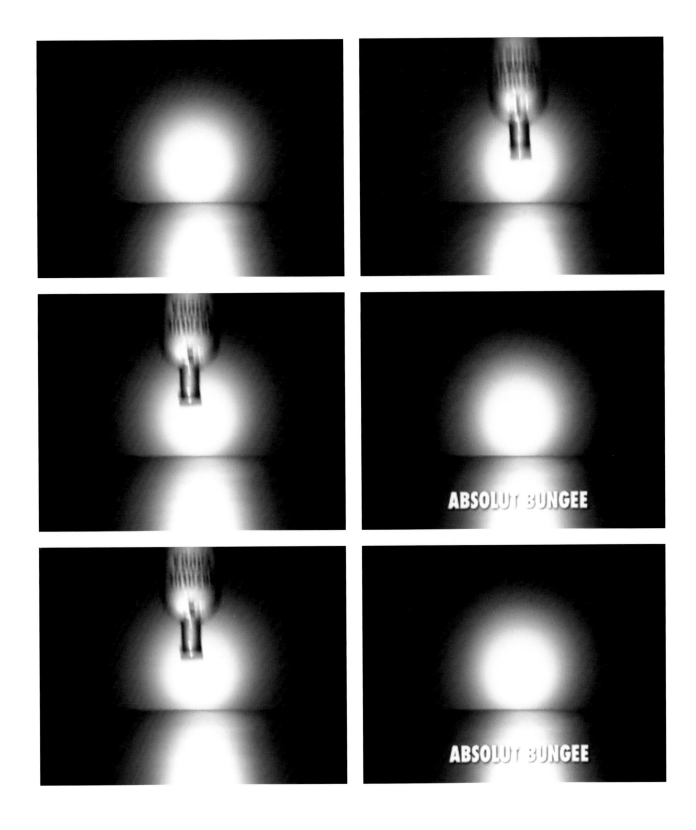

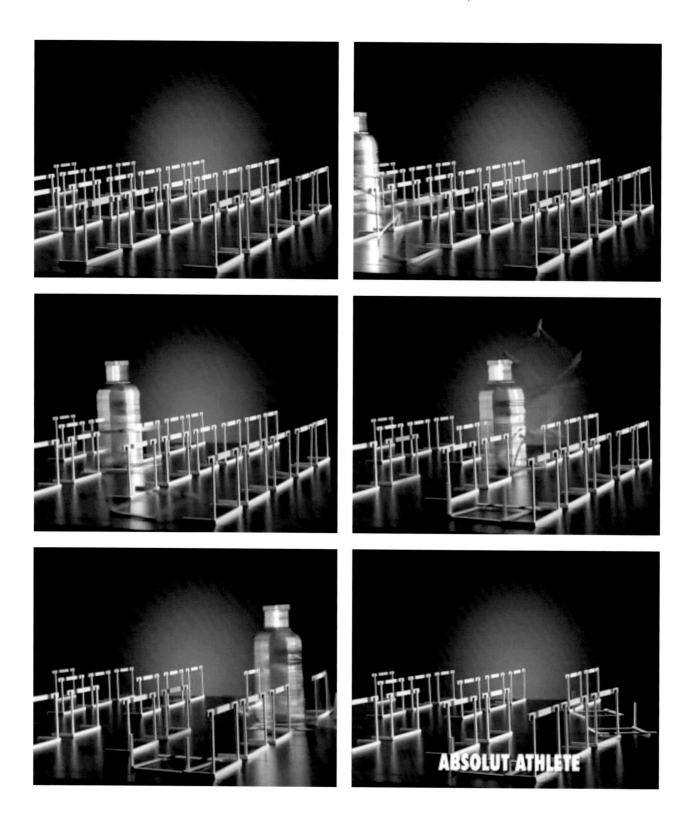

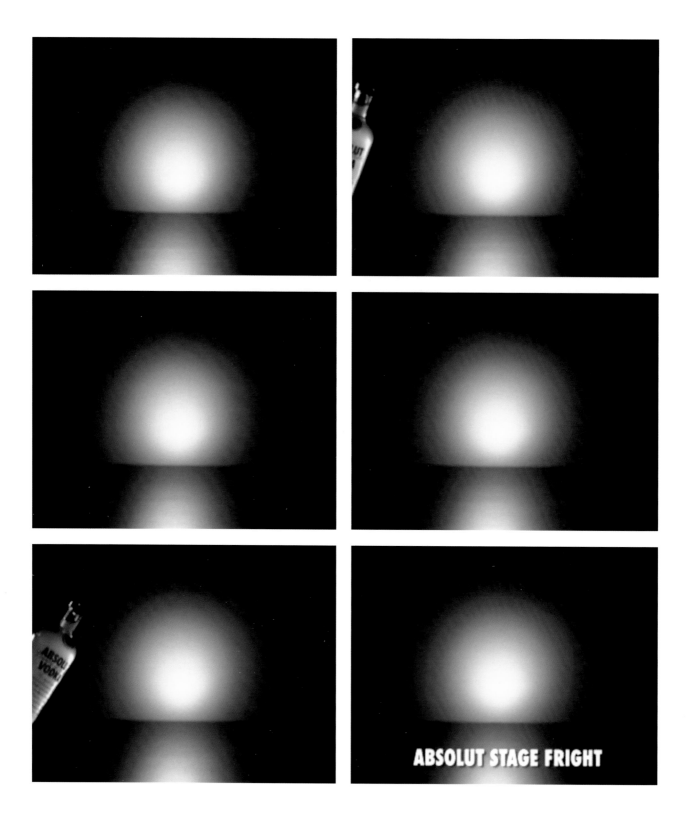

An ABSOLUT SEABREEZE is:

1 Part Absolut Vodka,
Cranberry juice,
2 Dashes Grapefruit juice.

Build over ice in a highball glass.
Garnish with an orange spiral.

absolut.com

REPLAY   VISIT SITE

PRINT RECIPE

ABSOLUT® VODKA PRODUCT OF SWEDEN.
40 AND 50% ALC/VOL (80 AND 100 PROOF).
100% GRAIN NEUTRAL SPIRITS. ABSOLUT
COUNTRY OF SWEDEN VODKA & LOGO, ABSOLUT,
ABSOLUT BOTTLE DESIGN, ABSOLUT CALLIGRAPHY
AND ABSOLUT.COM ARE TRADEMARKS OWNED BY
V&S VIN & SPRIT AB. ©2002 V&S VIN & SPRIT AB.
IMPORTED BY THE ABSOLUT SPIRITS CO.,
NEW YORK, NY.
ENJOY WITH ABSOLUT RESPONSIBILITY.

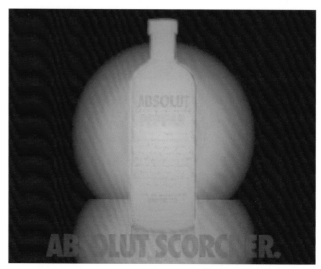

ABSOLUT FRESHNESS.

absolut.com

REPLAY **VISIT SITE**

TBWA ABSOLUT COUNTRY OF SWEDEN VODKA &
LOGO, ABSOLUT, ABSOLUT BOTTLE DESIGN AND
ABSOLUT CALLIGRAPHY ARE TRADEMARKS OWNED
BY V & S VIN & SPRIT AB.
© V & S VIN & SPRIT AB.
absolut.com

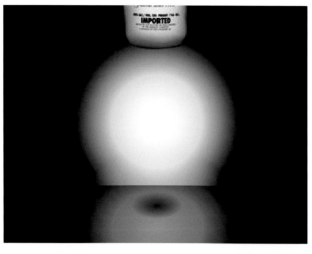

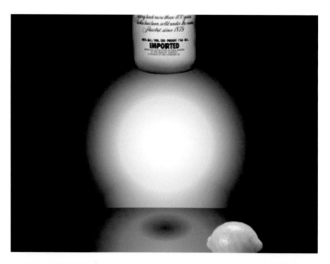

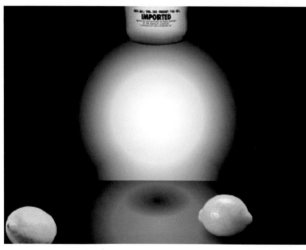

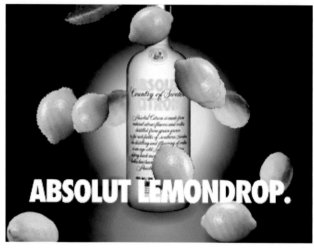

ABSOLUT LEMONDROP.

ABSOLUT LEMONDROP.

To make an ABSOLUT LEMONDROP:

Pour chilled ABSOLUT CITRON
into a shot glass.
Dip a wedge of lemon into sugar.
Drink and bite.

ABSOLUT LIMITATION

BANNER ADS: LIKE A STICK OF DENTYNE.

of the New York office's British invasion of 1999–2001, and is a true believer of the Internet's power to change the world.

He created a media planner/strategist team to tackle the "What next?" Absolut assignment. They were Micke Marticki and David Jacobson, two bright, earnest, young ad guys, seemingly inseparable, frequently bumping into walls and each other, as they tried to figure it out. To some extent, they, like many newcomers to the Absolut account, were intimidated by the past: the brand's (and the Agency's) success simply scared them. Week after week we reviewed their lengthy PowerPoint presentations. I began referring to them as Rosencrantz and Guildenstern, the two characters in Shakespeare's Hamlet who, assigned by Claudius to kill the prince, meet their own demise because they bumbled and bungled.

Doug Jaeger straightened this mess out. (And if I'm giving him too much credit he won't complain.) Up to then, banner ads were the only kind of ads available on Web sites that sold advertising. You know, they're the ads that look like sticks of Dentyne chewing gum. These were especially useless to Absolut as we were a "vertical" advertiser in our magazine ads, not a "horizontal" one. Doug knew that CNET had inaugurated a new ad size, actually a "box," that could accommodate our format. He figured if we maximized that space we could create entertaining ads that could serve multiple purposes. Visitors could play with an ad and then discover an Absolut recipe or be directed to absolut.com, Absolut's official Web site.

The secondary challenge would be to accomplish all this within the file-size limitations of the ads. I won't bore you with the details—it's sufficient if you understand that everything in a Web ad takes up valuable space, or memory: colors, sound, music, interaction, you name it. But the primary challenge was to make the ads fun, surprising, Absolut.

Every ad would begin with the bottle. Doug recalls this was ad insurance suggested by Carl Horton. He speculated if visitors didn't go on and play with the ad, at least they saw the bottle. Time, though, could be infinite. They could take as long as they wanted. He also figured we should reinvent some "old" ads and dress them up for the twenty-first century. Also, we weren't going to trick people, as tempting as that might be. If you rolled over an ad, or clicked on an object, you wouldn't suddenly find yourself in Neverland, captured by another Web site. We would be, as Pete Callaro might have said, honest Web citizens.

ABSOLUT LIMITATION The first ad to break reminded us why Absolut wasn't going to do banner ads in the first place.

Even Doug Jaeger couldn't do everything alone. He hired two guys, Dan Cronin and Jason Lucas, a writer/art director team from K2, a design firm inNew York. Dan's also a moonlighting comedian on the New York comedy club circuit; Jason plays the role of sidekick, but I suspect he's the real brains behind the operation. Together, they spun out dozens of entertaining ideas for what became an assignment to promote the flavors.

These guys really fulfilled the challenge: They created effective and award-winning ads, using the tools of the Net, and the spirit of the Absolut brand. I suppose without the false starts we wouldn't have had ultimate success. And by using the magazine campaign as a standard, we took out an insurance policy on the chance of embarrassing ourselves.

CHAIRMAN CARL

CARL HORTON IS CEO OF THE ABSOLUT SPIRITS COMPANY IN THE USA.

He has had a powerful impact on the Absolut advertising of the past decade, probably more than he realizes. Some days, he doesn't hate every idea. Carl, a Philadelphia native, is also a natural storyteller and like another Philadelphian, Bill Cosby, relishes expressing himself in a certain folksy manner. Sometimes it's harsh, sometimes it's sweet, but it's always Carl.

• Questioning a decision of his management on future direction:

"I'm trying to save you guys from yourselves."

• Acknowledging the choice of Cynthia Rowley for ABSOLUT COZY:

"She's one of the celebrity knitters of Chicago."

• "Great is wonderful, but . . ."

• "Allocation is just another way of sorting things."

• "Witty, my ass!"

• On hearing the news that one personality declined to be in ABSOLUT

ANNIVERSARY: "One monkey don't stop the show, baby!"

• "It's like tits on a bull."

• "Wherever you put it, there it is."

• "Let me tell you a wonderful story . . ."

• "Come back when you got something."

FASHIONISTAS

chapter thirteen

FROM THE MOMENT SUPERMODEL RACHEL WILLIAMS DONNED A SILVER LAMÉ minidress designed by David Cameron and leapt across a set photographed by Steven Meisel, Absolut and the public were hooked on ABSOLUT FASHION. ¶ Fashion is fun, particularly if you're not in the fashion business. Meaning, we got to play in the fashion world without the fashion world's worries: pleasing the real powers like Anna Wintour, editor of *Vogue*; the high-end department stores like Bloomingdales and Saks; the Wall Street and Main Street investors that launch, maintain, and disassemble fashion empires; and, of course, the fashion-buying public. We couldn't have a disastrous Fall Season because we had no Fall Season. We didn't have any smocks left over because we had none to begin with.

ABSOLUT VERSACE.

PHOTOGRAPHED BY HERB RITTS AT THE ICE HOTEL IN JUKKAS JÄRVI, SWEDEN.

ABSOLUT SPRING.

In celebration of Spring, Absolut Vodka and kate spade new york would like you to have this limited edition rain poncho.
Stay dry.

Instead, we could play dress-up like children at a tea party. We could lure the stars of the moment, or the era, to play with us because Absolut had created and polished an image as a brand with outstanding taste and cultural credentials. But backstage there was just a bunch of ad guys and clients who wanted to burnish the brand's image and have some fun.

ABSOLUT VERSACE The House of Versace has been in business since 1978. While I don't believe anyone has accused them of modesty, I think it's their sureness in the face of criticism and adversity that has kept them on their high-above perch. Absolut partnered with Versace in 1997. The plan was to create an American and European fashion insert for Vogue that would connect an aspect of Sweden's natural beauty with Versace's urban fashions. Also hatched by Daniel Gaujac, the TBWA account guy and impresario in Paris, the ad was shot in Jukkas Järvi, Sweden, home of the now famous Ice Hotel; starred Naomi Campbell and Kate Moss; and was photographed by Herb Ritts.

The Ice Hotel is an annual collaboration between man and nature. It is built out of ice (naturally) each November. Like Cinderella's coach, it melts the following April. In between, it's a functioning hotel, assuming you like sleeping on a slab of ice wearing triple underwear inside your steamy,

humidified sleeping bag. There's no electricity and no indoor plumbing. And if you have to pee during the night, it's quite an inconvenience. But it was an out-of-this-world setting for ABSOLUT VERSACE, not to mention a bone-chilling photo shoot in December, where the available light was available for only about four hours each day. (Summer's "Midnight Sun" has its winter opposite: "Darkness at Noon.")

However, with a mighty assist from then publisher Ron Gallotti, Conde Nast's version of Billy Martin, the New York Yankees' always departing, always returning manager, and the very classy and lovely Marsha Mossack, *Vogue*'s creative director, the supermodels found their way to Sweden and stayed long enough to shiver through a memorable shoot.

ABSOLUT SPRING Kate Spade was a newly minted fashion star in 1998. Her stuff, especially her simple but classy handbags, with the little "kate spade" labels on the outside, were must-haves. A Midwesterner (Kansas City, actually) in upbringing and demeanor, Kate Spade brought a sensibility and classiness to the New York fashion world. Of course, I didn't know any of this, but Kitty Hall did; she told me and I naturally believed her. And we actually had an "in" at her company: Andy Spade, her husband, was a former writer at Chiat/Day. Our idea was to commission Kate to

an enclosed area where dancers were doused with a steady stream of soapsuds to help lubricate their activities. Many of the models were dressed in just their underwear, another sign that their clothes were being laundered. Plus there was no shortage of feathers, beads, rhinestones, and an Absolut fingernail here and there.

ABSOLUT LEGENDS

Sweden is a country whose citizens are very much in touch with Nature. Everyone, seemingly, has a summer-house away from Stockholm. Or even better, they own an island in the archipelago of thousands of islands.

While vacationing at these homes, Swedes contemplate and celebrate a spiritual and myth-filled past dominated by eight legends. Probably the most famous, and certainly the most glorious, is that of Midsommar. This is the celebration of the first night of summer, after the loooong and darrrrk winter. The sun literally doesn't set. Everything in nature comes to life and is imbued with supernatural powers. Young maidens wander through the meadows picking flowers, which they place beneath their pillows to help them dream about their future husbands. This is certainly a lot more romantic than an Internet dating service.

Or consider Midsommar's seasonal opposite: Lucia. Lucia arrives on the winter's eve, to bring hope and light for the future. Dressed in virginal white and red-belted, Lucia recalls her martyr's death by wearing a crown of lighted candles, a symbol of her faith. Yet, her eye sockets bleed because she has surrendered her own eyes to her lover.

Jean-Paul Gaultier interpreted these legends, designing original, almost current fashions for each. Then Jean-Baptiste Mondino photographed them at Sandhamn, in the Stockholm archipelago. Joining Midsommar and Lucia, were Näcken, the virtuoso violinist; Oxdans, the fighter of the mating bulls; Älva, the enchanting dancer; Viking, the conqueror of the Seven Seas; Valkyria, who whisks battlefield heroes to Valhalla; and my favorite, Valborg, who signals the arrival of spring: a night of sorcery, witches brooming off to Black Mountain for a dance with the Devil, bonfires, cowbells, and other peace-disturbing implements.

design a rain poncho, featuring Absolut bottles as rain-drops, as a consumer give-away for the first day of spring. Spade actually liked the idea. Laura Stoddardt, a Londoner, created the artwork of the little girl under the umbrella.

ABSOLUT TOM FORD As of this writing, Tom Ford is best known—and deservedly damn well known—as the designer who turned around the leather goods company Gucci during the 1990s. Serving as "creative director" alongside president Domenico de Sole, he took what was acknowledged to be a moribund brand—Gucci—and reinvented it as a billion-dollar fashion empire in Tom Ford's own image: sexy, racy, and imaginative—an often brilliant force in the fashion world. Unfortunately, this corporate marriage fell apart in 2004 when Gucci was purchased by Pinault-Printemps-Redoute (PPR), and Tom Ford and Domenico de Sole abruptly departed for points unknown.

Five years earlier, during Ford's heyday, Absolut teamed up with Gucci for an eight-page ad photographed by Mario Testino. Testino was fresh from London with his jaw wired shut due to a fall on the ice. *Vogue* magazine, once again, played fashion Cupid. The associate publisher, Edward Menicheschi, (50/50 chance I've got the spelling correct), brought all the parties together for a shoot in a suburban Paris discotheque. Its main attraction, which we took full advantage of, was the "Laundromat" zone. This was actually

ABSOLUT COZY While Absolut hasn't gotten around to dressing poodles, we have dressed things besides people. For instance, we've dressed the Absolut bottle. For Christmas 2001, Cynthia Rowley, a designer from Chicago, created a woolly cozy for Absolut. Cozies typically cover teapots to keep them warm and you-know-what. This cozy was distributed to hundreds of thousands of readers of the *New*

LUCIA, BRINGS LIGHT TO THE DARKEST NIGHT

ÄLVA, THE ENCHANTING DANCER IN THE MIST

VIKING, CONQUEROR OF THE SEVEN SEAS

VALKYRIA, THE BEAUTIFUL GODDESS OF THE BATTLEFIELDS

VALBORG, THE FIRE THAT CHASES EVIL SPIRITS AWAY

ABSOLUT GAULTIER.

ABSOLUT AND OTHER FAMOUS SWEDISH LEGENDS, AS SEEN BY JEAN PAUL GAULTIER AND JEAN-BAPTISTE MONDINO
AT SANDHAMN, IN THE ARCHIPELAGO OF STOCKHOLM, SWEDEN.
absolut.com/legends

York Times and *Chicago Tribune* inside their Sunday paper. A sweater Rowley's grandfather created for a beer commercial when he was an advertising art director inspired the cozy design. Surely, it was a tasty, high quality beer.

ABSOLUT STELLA When Stella McCartney entered the Agency's St. Pat's Conference Room (the windows face St. Patrick's Cathedral), she examined the wall of Absolut album covers that welcomed her. Walking across the room she eyed David Bowie, Velvet Underground, the Sex Pistols, and Miles Davis. At each ad she nodded, and said, "Got that." When she approached the final cover, John and Yoko's Two Virgins, Stella exclaimed, "No, not this one!"

Stella McCartney is, of course, the daughter of ex-Beatle Paul McCartney. More relevantly, she's a fashion designer in the Gucci empire, with boutiques in New York and London. Some would describe McCartney's fashions as possessing amusing sensuality. See, I just did. And between not taking herself too seriously—as a person or designer— yet, also creating fashions with an unabashed femininity, she was a natural Absolut partner. The Absolut garments were modeled by Tetyana Brazhnyk and drawn by David Remfry, a New York artist, at a closed session in London.

Stella's rock star genes don't hurt either. ABSOLUT STELLA was introduced at a party at the infamous L.A. hotel, Chateau Marmont. It was attended by luminaries such as Steve Martin, (father) Paul, Leo DiCaprio, Tobey McGuire, and Chloe Sevigny. But the hotel is so dark in places I had difficulty spotting the stars. I just tried to avoid literally bumping into the walls.

ABSOLUT SADIST.

BONJOUR/BONSOIR

chapter fourteen

WELL, THAT'S IT FOR ME.

When I first reported for work at TBWA (pre-Chiat\Day) in February, 1987, I had no idea what lay ahead. I was a bit in awe. I was skinny back then, had most of my hair, and still suffered from a case of youthful optimism. (Now I suffer from middle-aged optimism.) I knew this was a job at a feisty New York agency run by an ambitious and complicated Greek-American, Bill Tragos. Bill had the nerve to grow up in St. Louis, Missouri, begin an ad career in New York, follow it to Europe at Young & Rubicam, found his own agency network in Paris, and then return to New York to make it big on his home soil. His only warning to me: "Lewis, don't screw it up."

His counterpart at the client, Carillon Importers, was Michel Roux: a French paratrooper, a Texas salesman, a New York marketing genius—maybe even in that order.

Together, they powered an agency/client partnership as famous for its longevity as its success, but built on doing things their way. They didn't need McKinsey. They didn't need dopey marketing jargon to be inspired to break the rules, to think out of the box. (What box?) They didn't need a few housewives in New Jersey to ratify their ideas in focus groups. (No offense to any New Jersey housewives. It's just an expression.)

They did believe in bringing smart, creative, and passionate people together to take chances, walk in fresh footprints, and particularly in Michel's case, have fun along the way. (Bill always looks a little guilty when he's having fun.) And maybe build a multi-billion dollar brand, too.

Roll the clock forward seventeen years: it's time for someone else to have the fun. (Neal, are you having fun yet?) Not to mention, the world has changed, and maybe, just maybe, ABSOLUT —————, two words and the photo of a vodka bottle endlessly role-playing, may no longer be the only answer. But don't let your mother—or your children—throw anything "Absolut" away. I hear there's a market for these ads.

As for me, I plan to dabble. After nearly two decades of absolutism, I'm very ready to try fifty other things. But make no mistake: I will continue to drink Absolut gimlets (on the rocks) and I have preordered my headstone. You can pretty much guess what shape it is.

CREATIVE DIRECTORS

timeline

HERE, ALL TOGETHER, ARE THE AGENCY AND ABSOLUT CREATIVE DIRECTORS in New York, as I have reassembled them. The dates, if not precise, are very close. If you were a creative director and were somehow omitted, sorry, get over it.

TBWA

Carole Anne Fine	Arnie Arlow	Peter Lubalin	Tony DeGregorio
1977–1982	*1982–1994*	*1982–1994*	*1994–1997*

Marty Cooke	Eric McClellan	Jerry Gentile	Bob Kuperman
1996–1997	*1997–1998*	*1998*	*1999–2000*

David Page	Dallas Itzen	Patrick O'Neill	Gerry Graf
2000–2001	*2001–2003*	*2001–2003*	*2004–*

ABSOLUT

Geoff Hayes	Dan Braun	Joseph Mazzafero	Patrick O' Neill
1980–1987, 1993–1997	*1998–1999*	*1999-2003*	*2002-2005*

ACKNOWLEDGMENTS

An advertising campaign is generally the collaboration of many talented people, most of them rowing in the same direction. This book contains their stories, at least to the extent they impacted what *Advertising Age* named the "7ᵀᴴ Best Campaign of the 20ᵀᴴ Century." (Who said smart-asses can't finish in the Top 10?)

But there's a handful of people behind the scenes, inside and outside the Agency, that deserve a special mention:

MICHAEL PERSSON at Absolut, Sweden. If he didn't think this book was a good idea, it never would have happened. He's more than a good client; he's a good friend.

BILLY ALBORES heads art buying at TBWA\Chiat\Day. One of Billy's great talents is to convince people to do things they don't want to do, at a price they don't want to do it, and then be happy with the results. If you think that's hard to understand, imagine how difficult it is to do.

NANCY KIM was my assistant extraordinaire, before, during and after I wrote this book. Yet she also had time to be a snap Account Executive, too. And while she's still figuring out if Advertising is her "calling," (me, too) she did a great job making me look good.

CHRISTINA WALL was a 2004 summer intern at the Agency. She lucked out when she was assigned to Absolut. I lucked out, as she became my human Google, fact-finding and fact-checking everything under the sun. She was an absolute cannonball, and a fun one.

My friend SCHWAMY: When I was hurling through the Universe on some uncharted flight, he brought me back to Earth, largely intact.

ISABEL is my wife. As the expression goes, she puts up with a lot. After 28 years, she's still trying to figure out when I am crazy and when I'm merely acting crazy.

ABSOLUT ADS

INDEX

ABSOLUT ADS

CONTINUED